DATE DUE

JUN 17 '81			
FEB 23 '82			

THE AMERICAN TOUCH
IN MICRONESIA

★ THE
AMERICAN TOUCH
IN
MICRONESIA

by DAVID NEVIN

W · W · NORTON & COMPANY · INC

New York

Published simultaneously in Canada by George J. McLeod Limited, Toronto. Printed in the United States of America.

First Edition

LIBRARY OF CONGRESS CATALOGING IN PUBLICATION DATA

Nevin, David, 1927–
   The American touch in Micronesia.

   Bibliography: p.
   Includes index.
   1. Micronesia—Politics and government.
2. Micronesia—Economic policy.   3. Micronesia—Social
policy.   4. United States—Insular possessions.
I. Title.
JQ6451.A3N48   1977   309.1'96'5   76-58339
ISBN 0 393 05617 1

1 2 3 4 5 6 7 8 9 0

To the hard-pressed educators of Micronesia

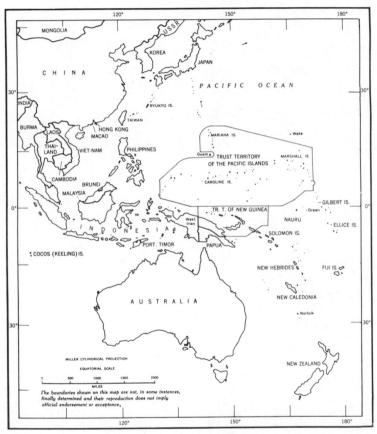

Micronesia and the Far Pacific

CONTENTS

ACKNOWLEDGMENTS

As the dedication of this book suggests, my greatest debt in its preparation is to the educators of Micronesia. Of the two hundred interviews which are its basic source, more than half are with educators there who gave unreservedly of their time and assistance and personal warmth. It would trouble me if they were to see this book as an attack on their efforts, since in fact they struggle valiantly to keep up with the demands of their clients in a situation which is not of their making. And I doubt that they will quarrel with my findings. Still, *The American Touch in Micronesia* may not please all quarters of officialdom, and since retaliation is easy in a closed place like Micronesia, I shall not list names beyond the few who gave me unusual assistance and whom I judge fully secure. They include, in no particular order, John Perkins, then of Yap; Alfonso Oiterong of Palau; David Ramarui of Palau and Saipan, director of education; Kinja Andrike of Majuro in the Marshalls; Peggy Bennett, then of Palau; Chutomu Nimwes of Truk; Calvin Snodgrass of Majuro; and Terry Edvalson of Ponape.

I am particularly indebted to Dirk A. Ballendorf, former Peace Corps official and the most knowledgeable man on Micronesia whom I have encountered in the United States. In addition to assistance on many levels, he read and commented on the completed manuscript.

Joseph Oakey, then deputy director of education in the Trust Territory, served as host for my trip, opened all the doors, and made no attempt to guide the results.

Dr. Saul Riesenberg of the Smithsonian Institution, who has devoted his life to the anthropology of Pacific peoples, read an early version of Chapter Two and made suggestions; the errors that it and the rest of the book may contain are, of course, my own. Dr. Leonard Mason, professor emeritus of anthropology at the University of Hawaii, spent a long afternoon talking with me in a Honolulu hotel lobby while nearby a group of tourists labored through hula lessons.

In Washington, Janice Johnson of the Office of Territories, Department of Interior, who is one of the Trust Territories' key supporters, always gave me generous assistance and support from the beginning of my study to its end. William R. Tansill of the Congressional Research Service of the Library of Congress, the Capitol Hill expert on Micronesia, generously saw me through that institution's holdings on Micronesia. Lola Smith made me understand the real qualities of the Pacific Islands Central School.

Three Americans in Micronesia gave me particular help. Dr. William Vitarelli, a salty visionary, shared his unique views. Father Francis Hezel of Truk understands education as well as anyone in the islands. Dr. Robert Fisher, director of mental health and the first psychiatrist to work in Micronesia, gave me invaluable insights.

Among the many and varied contributions of my wife, Luciana Colla Nevin, was the book's title.

Finally, for sending me to Micronesia in the first place,

for encouraging me without stint to turn my original report into the book, and for assisting the book in various other critical ways, I am grateful to the Ford Foundation, and to Edward J. Meade Jr., Harold Howe II, and most particularly, Ralph G. Bohrson.

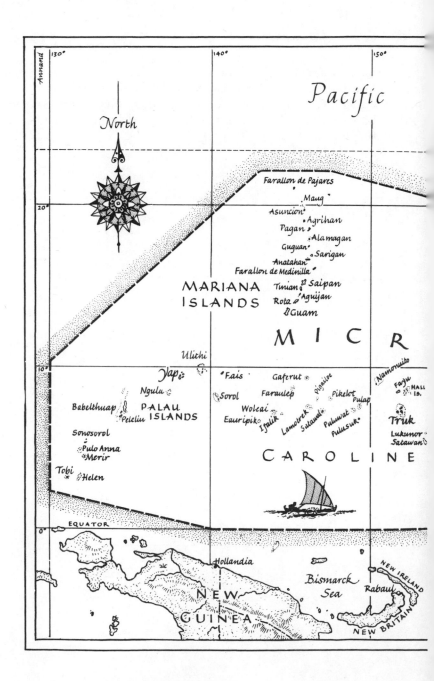

Annand

130°   140°   150°

North

Pacific

Farallon de Pajares
Maug
Asuncion
Agrihan
Pagan
Alamagan
Guguan
Sarigan
Anatahan
Farallon de Medinilla

MARIANA   Tinian   Saipan
ISLANDS   Rota   Aguijan
           Guam

MICR

20°

10°

Ulithi

Yap   Fais   Gaferut   Namonuito
Ngulu   Sorol   Faraulep   Pigailoe   Faju   HALL IS.
Babelthuap PALAU   Woleai   Pikelot Pulap
Peleliu ISLANDS Eauripik Ifalik Lamotrek Satawal Puluwat Truk
Sonsorol   Satawal Pulusuk   Lukunor
Pulo Anna   Satawan
Merir
Tobi Helen   CAROLINE

EQUATOR

0°

Hollandia   Bismarck   NEW IRELAND
                             Sea   Rabaul
        NEW
        GUINEA   NEW BRITAIN

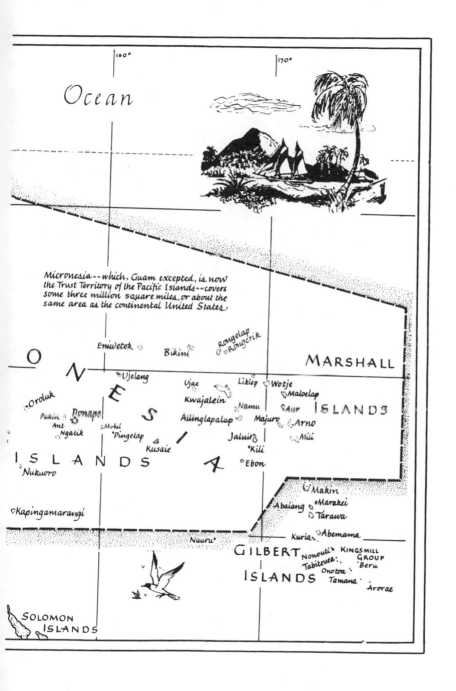

Ocean

160°   170°

Micronesia -- which, Guam excepted, is now
the Trust Territory of the Pacific Islands--covers
some three million square miles, or about the
same area as the continental United States

O   N   Eniwetok   Bikini   Rongelap
                                               Rongerik

                                                        MARSHALL
                    Ujelang   Ujae   Likiep   Wotje
Oroluk   Kwajalein   Maloelap
                                         Namu   Jaur   ISLANDS
Puluot   Ponape   Allinglapalap   Majuro   Arno
Ant   Mokil   Jaluit   Mili
Ngatik   Pingelap   Kili
            Kusaie   A   Ebon
ISLANDS
Nukuoro

Kapingamarangi   Makin
                                Abaiang   Marakei
                                           Tarawa
                    Nauru   Kuria   Abemama
                              GILBERT   Nonouti   KINGSMILL
                                        Tabiteuea   GROUP
                                        Onotoa   Beru
                              ISLANDS   Tamana
                                                Arorae

SOLOMON
ISLANDS

INTRODUCTION

This is a book about Americans in Micronesia and the strange and dangerous sense of unreality that their policies have created. It is only incidentally about Micronesians themselves. I have described Micronesians and their beautiful islands only so much as necessary to explore generally the nature of life on a small island, which I think is fundamental to an understanding of the disaster wrought there.

I am not prescribing what Micronesians should do or should be or what they should want. I don't know what future they should have or may have. I don't know any Americans who know. I don't even know any Micronesians who know. Like the rest of the world, they will have to work out their destiny in the context of the reality they encounter. My guess is that the working out process will be very rough and that if all the Micronesians I met survive, they will be lucky. If their free institutions survive, that will be even luckier.

That also is the conviction that emboldens me to write this book. Americans have had a disastrous impact on Micronesia. They have been motivated by their interest in the strategic value of the islands and have been guided by a naive altruism and an arrogant assumption of superiority that has allowed no self-questioning. If Micronesians do not fully recognize themselves in this book, I believe that the Americans involved will find themselves readily. They are my subject.

This is a journalistic book. It is based on more than two hundred interviews in Washington, San Francisco, Honolulu, Guam, and in all six districts of Micronesia. (Kusaie had not become a separate district when I was there and I did not visit it.) Every quotation used is drawn directly from an interview except when another source is clearly indicated.

The work began when the Ford Foundation engaged me as a consultant to examine education in Micronesia and to prepare a background report that would help it evaluate a grant it was contemplating there. I quickly found that one could not view education other than in the context of—and as a primary cause of—the fog of unreality that has arisen around the American administration of the islands. My report dwelt as much on the society as on its schools, and the decision to proceed with this book followed naturally.

In its preparation I have expanded my original research, especially in developing the activities of the United States in Micronesia in the early 1960s, when the decision was made to begin pouring in money. It was this money, moving primarily through the schools, that created the dilemma of unreality that now afflicts the islands.

This story had never been put together. I drew it from the record and from the participants, and it was so complex that many of the participants were surprised at what the record revealed. None knew the whole story. All of them, even those most directly involved, are likely to be surprised at the full account.

This original story can be seen as small, for it involved relatively few people and relatively small sums of money injected into a distant part of the world. But I believe that it is fundamentally important for what it says of Micronesia and of the trouble that lies ahead—and for what it says of the nature of America in the 1960s.

D.N.

Do not open me, otherwise;
under other circumstances,
protect yourself from the owners.

—*Sign on a locker,*
Marshall Islands High School
Majuro

★
★ ★ CHAPTER ONE
★

DISASTER IN THE MAKING

The islands of Micronesia are scattered across the western Pacific like stars across the night, and when you visit them you are struck immediately by their beauty and perfection. It is only later, after you have been there awhile and listened to many people and sorted out the discord between their desires and their capacity for realizing those desires, that you begin to understand the trouble that lies ahead like a tropical thunderhead. It is a peculiarly American sort of trouble, for Micronesia is the last American colony. The dangers that await it are clearly marked "Made in U. S. A."

There are some two thousand of these islands, including the Marianas, the Eastern and Western Carolines, and the Marshalls, with a total land area of only a few hundred square miles. Since a few are sizeable, most are tiny. The outermost islands are scattered three thousand miles along the equator (2° to 20° north), from slightly west of Honolulu to within five hundred miles of the Philippines.

Some are high islands, volcanic mountains clad in rain forests that thrust up into clouds which split and pour waterfalls back to the sea. Most are low islands—coral flecks linked in atolls around a lagoon—with a coral reef alive with brilliant fish. The great swells of the Pacific run before the trades for thousands of miles in such orderly rhythm that knowing men can navigate by them. The island is only a momentary anomaly in their path. But on the beach, shaken by the breaking waves—the marks of crabs and birds and men washed away twice each day by the renewing tide—there is a serene aloneness in the immense sea. The world is here, the horizons are empty, and men fit the island and live by its rhythm. The brilliant fish about the reef are sweet as the fruit hanging heavy in the trees. The coconut palm grows wherever the sea hurls its nuts. It is the staff of life, for it always gives fresh water. Even in an era of ice and beer, a green drinking-coconut fresh from the tree, its top lopped with a machete stroke, is the brightest draught on the island. The sun is warming and the sea breeze cooling; man is in harmony and the living is easy.

So is the image of perfection. Americans and Europeans from the cold latitudes have been coming here for four hundred years and calling it paradise. If man could recreate Eden, it might emerge as a Pacific island.

But perfection is illusion, and today reality is destroying illusions in Micronesia with increasing speed. Now the trouble lies so near that the edges of Micronesian society are beginning to crumble. For perfect as the islands may be in isolation, they are poorly equipped to function in the modern world. And their sun-browned people, having tasted the pleasures, conveniences, comforts, and intellectual expansion of the modern world, want to leave their perfect shell-age islands for the twentieth century. In itself, that isn't new—throughout the underdeveloped world people want out of stone-age isolation and into cities, and most find the passage perilous.

The vastly complicating difference in Micronesia, how-

ever, is the American patron. The last of a long chain of
foreign meddlers, the U. S. has had by far the greatest effect. Magellan was the first European known to have landed
in Micronesia, and Spain held the islands for more then 350
years. Late in the last century Germany took over most of
them, and the United States acquired Guam. In 1914 Japan
quietly ousted the Germans and took everything but Guam;
its control eventually was formalized by the Treaty of Versailles, which led to a League of Nations mandate. As
World War II began, Japan also seized Guam. In 1944, beating its way up the Pacific toward Japan proper, the United
States took all the Micronesian islands in a series of bloody
battles. It has held them ever since. In 1947 the United Nations declared Micronesia a trust territory, with the United
States as trustee. Thus all of Micronesia except Guam,
which is a territory of the United States, is known as the
Trust Territory of the Pacific Islands.

For almost twenty years the United States excluded visitors (just as Japan had done) and put as little money as possible into the administration of the Trust Territory. The
unrealistic intent was to keep everything dormant, with the
U.S. military in firm control. In the early 1960s, however,
the United States changed its policy and began pouring relatively huge sums of money into the islands. There is nothing mysterious about American motives. Its interest in the
islands has been entirely strategic—and it intends to keep
the islands. But under the terms of the United Nations
trust, it must do so, more or less, through the free-will acceptance of the people of Micronesia. During the Kennedy
Administration, acting on a plan formulated in the National
Security Council, the United States set out to win Micronesia's hand with that essentially American bouquet, a fistful
of money. It planned to build up the islands until the people there would be so delighted with the U.S. role that they
would vote themselves readily into a premanent relationship with their benefactors.

That it has not worked that way is no surprise. What is

surprising are the problems our insertion of money has created. Obviously our move was self-interested. But the men who made it also saw it as beneficial to the recipients, and indeed, as another sign that Americans were just a bit more noble, generous, and far-sighted than the rest of the world's peoples. That was a popular myth of the period.

For more than a decade we have been pouring money into Micronesia without any consideration of its impact. Year after year, something like $600 per man, woman, and child has entered an economy which at the beginning of the period depended largely on subsistence and barter. Naturally it has produced immense change in the way people live and has created attitudes and expectations that bear almost no relation to the realities of life in Micronesia.

For the reality is that in Micronesia the term developing nation is a hollow compliment—so little is there to develop. Pardise turns out to be particularly ill equipped to supply the raw materials and systems and manufactures that make modern success. Furthermore, the cultural patterns of subsistence life in paradise turn out to be very poorly fitted to the organized, structured, scheduled modern world. The basic Micronesian attitudes toward work, family, and society are almost the opposite of what the technical west expects in its workers.

Into this dangerously anomalous situation the American money has poured willy-nilly, following the easiest paths and those most likely to produce the quickest measurements of tangible progress—which has usually meant building and hiring. There has been almost no consideration of how Micronesia would live in the long run, or how it would maintain the structure that foreign money was raising and foreign bureaucrats were directing. This follows readily from the reality of the American presence: no master plan for Micronesian development appeared because the expansion was not done for Micronesia's long-range benefit; it was done for America's short-range benefit. Furthermore, the U.S. imperative always was different than traditional colonial patterns. Its interest was not economic but strategic and thus concerned with countries other than Micronesia. So there was no particular reason to notice what was happening around it; in its strategic control, America was getting what it wanted.

At the same time, the United States has consciously frozen out other influences. By barring visitors for years, and by barring foreign trade until 1974, the United States alone has shepherded Micronesia into the modern world. As a result, it has provided the only role model available for the people there. Through the money it inserted, it also has supplied the illusion of the wherewithall to support that role model. Thus one of the least developed nations on earth has been encouraged to see itself in terms of the richest, most highly developed nation on earth.

But with all its money and success, the United States has created nothing in Micronesia by which the people can support the lifestyle they have been taught to see as their due. This is not to say, of course, that it is only because of the American example that Micronesians want to leave their shell-age islands and enter the modern world. People do not want to stand still in an interacting world, nor should they. American officials, increasingly discomfited by the results of their largesse now try to shift the responsibility by saying that people should not be expected to accept a life limited to picking coconuts, when all around them the world beckons. But like so many exculpatory arguments, this one avoids the issue.

The issue is that the Micronesians have been offered a world that bears almost no relationship to their own capacities. They have acquired the tastes and expectations of a modern western technological society, but their resources remain comparable to those of the poorest Asian nations. The result is a striking and pervasive unreality which affects every aspect of life in the islands. It colors the way people think, what they expect, how they conduct themselves.

This unreality is the real trouble in Micronesia. It is at the heart of the Micronesian dilemma. And it is so pervasive that it occurred to me, as I moved from island to island and found the same attitudes everywhere, that were an individual to act on the assumptions and unrealities that here govern a whole society, he might well be considered insane.

This is an American problem. We have used the Micronesians and changed them for our larger world purposes, and in the simplest terms of justice, we have made ourselves responsible for them. This is so clear that Micronesian nationalists—a new and distrubing reaction to the dilemma—believe today that they were the victims of a conscious American conspiracy to create a situation in which Micronesia could never stand alone and thus would be bound to the patron nation's strategic needs. This conclusion is all based on effects, working backwards from what has happened. There is neither evidence of a conspiracy nor reason to believe one exists—even considering the secret recommendations of a presidential commission on ways to influence a Micronesian plebiscite in favor of the United States. But given the results America has achieved, there might as well have been a conspiracy. Indeed, one might be more confident of American wisdom (if not its decency) had there been one. Instead, the Micronesian disaster seems to have been worked by simple incompetence.

And I realized with some horror that next to money in responsibility is the school system, erected like everything else on American lines—a weak academic model you might find in any little American town where budgets are low and the superintendent is about to be fired. Education is supposed to solve problems—but in this world of unreal expectations and bloated self-images, education is the instigator of unreality, having both shaped and compounded the dilemma.

Nor was this an accident. Education was the consciously chosen instrument by which the United States decided to make its impact on Micronesia. "The accelerated program that is contemplated will place great emphasis on education," said President John F. Kennedy in a formal statement on July 20, 1962, "for, in our opinion, education is the key to all further progress—political, economic and social." He looked for, he said, "striking improvement of education at all levels in the Trust Territory, upgrading education to a level comparable to the level which has been taken for granted in the United States for decades."[*]

In only a couple of sentences, Kennedy thus managed to spell out the American assumptions and attitudes that have proved so disastrous in Micronesia—and to tie them firmly to education.

Education is by far the most ubiquitous presence of government and of American influence. Since Kennedy's message it always has had the largest operating budget in government. It puts more money into the economy, hires more people, has more arms and more clients, affects more families, and touches more lives than anything short of American money itself.

Furthermore, education symbolizes the American presence. In its expenditures, its lack of imagination, its reproduction of a mediocre American urban system, its refusal to adjust itself to Micronesian terrain and culture, its lack of forethought, its essential failure, and the likelihood of its impending collapse (for educationally, just as in the society itself, things plainly are going from bad to worse), it stands for how we have handled Micronesia.

And through the money it spends, the content it projects, the expectations it fosters, the grandiose self-images it spawns in students and in their parents, and the role models it imposes on the society, education surely has outstripped every other institution in Micronesia in creating attitudes and expectations that are simply unreal.

But it is too much to paint education as an action arm of U.S. policy. It is, like the money itself, much more an unwitting tool. Indeed, education can be seen as victim as well

[*] Public Papers of the Presidents, John F. Kennedy, 1962 (Washington D.C.: Government Printing Office, 1963), pp. 564–565.

as instigator of the unreality that is the dilemma of Micronesia. It is victim in that the people's lack of understanding of the society that has arisen, their newly formed desires and ambitions, goad education along, never quite giving it time to regroup and reorient itself and plumb for proper directions. And it is instigator in that the effect of education (no matter the anguished reservations of many educators) is to move the people it serves along a preordained course that exacerbates the problem and certainly is the wrong course—no matter what the right course may turn out to be.

Left to themselves, Micronesians would have entered the twentieth century in different ways, perhaps better and perhaps worse, but at least theirs. As it happened, the American presence came with a predisposed mindset which education begins to instill in every child at age six. The controlling metropolitan power casually models the future on itself without even wondering if there are alternatives.

That is why my experience in Micronesia led me directly to a critique of the society. I went to look at schools, but what I saw was a society in trouble.

We have educated these people, at least slightly, and that is the easy part. But we have done nothing about the hard part, which is to create an economic structure in which they can use a modern western academic education.

To put it more starkly, expectations in Micronesia have risen so far beyond the possibility of satisfying them as to destroy hope, and hope destroyed is the root of social misery. Thus grows the potential disaster which now faces America on these idyllic islands on the other side of the world, this angry, sullen, frightened paradise in the western Pacific.

I met Father Francis Hezel, principal of Xavier, a Catholic high school, on a splendid beach on the island of Moen in the Truk Lagoon. It was Sunday and he had brought the senior class on a party. The beach was near a hotel and miles from the school. He had chosen it, on an island ringed by beaches where the diving is famous around the world, because it was one of the few places not contaminated by sewage. Hezel, not yet forty, is a lean, muscled man and a powerful swimmer. He led the way out to a visiting yacht, and we clung to the anchor chain in the warm water while the yachtsmen above studiously ignored us. When the party was over, Hezel took the class back to the school, and at dusk he drove back to the hotel for dinner with me.

On the way the headlights of the school's old truck picked up a man in the road with a machete. As the truck passed, the man swung the big blade at Hezel's head. Hezel jerked back from the window and the blade clattered on the door. Hezel is a Jesuit, as are most priests in Micronesia. Perhaps he would have been a marine had he not been a priest, which is not inconsistent with his order. Hezel stopped the truck and got out. The man cocked the machete back, waiting. He was drunk, of course, but not at all unsteady. Hezel had an idea he could come in under the machete and take the man, beat him with the flat of his own blade, throw him in the truck, and deliver him to the police.

But the last time he had done that it had not worked so well. He had seen a man on the side of the road, drunk as always, hurl a rock the size of a coconut through the windshield of a car that crept along the bumpy road. He did this again before Hezel subdued him and took him to the police station. But perhaps he had a family member there, for he was released as soon as Hezel left. Or maybe the police disliked the idea of an American—priest or not—arresting a Trukese for any reason. The concept of police, and for that matter, the concept of justice itself in its western form, are not all that workable in Micronesia.

So Hezel thought better of the whole matter, got back into his truck, and came to dinner. He was still angry and a bit shaken when he arrived. But that is the way things go on the island of Moen at Truk and in many other places in Micronesia. There are many drunks and it is considered better not to be abroad at night, especially for Americans.

"They're such beautiful people," Hezel said, "the kids, you know, they smile and they're so open and warm and joyous, until they're about fifteen, and then something seems to close down on them. Some light goes out. You don't see so many smiles after they're about fifteen." That may be particularly true at Truk, where conditions are most advanced in Micronesia, but it is certain that there are a great many unhappy people on these idyllic islands in the western Pacific.

Micronesia could not exist in its current state without the U.S. treasury. There are many indications of this, but two basic figures particularly demonstrate the frightening disparity between what Micronesia spends and what it earns. These figures are the benchmarks of an ill society.

The current American contribution to the Trust Territory budget is about $66 million a year, a pittance in U.S. government terms, but a fortune when spread among 112,000 people who have grown from a subsistence heritage. The money accounts for more than 90 percent of the Trust Territory budget of about $72 million. While the total budget figure includes some $5 million raised locally, the source for most of that $5 million is income taxes paid on salaries which are paid from the $66 million, and business taxes that come largely from the same source. Thus, directly and indirectly, the United States not only supports Micronesia—in effect, it *is* Micronesia's fiscal life. There are estimates—and no one really knows—that in real terms the United States supplies about 98 percent of Micronesia's funding. That is a startling figure for a land that is throwing off a subsistence lifestyle in favor of a money economy.

The second frightening figure is the growth of Micronesia's imports when cast against its static and even shrinking exports. Micronesia's only real product is copra, coconut meat that has dried in the sun and is sold, usually in Japan, for its oil. Each year copra provides more than half Micronesia's export total. Otherwise there is a pitifully small—a disgracefully small—fishing industry; some vegetables sold to American military bases at Guam and Kwajalein; a tiny handicraft industry; some trochus shell sold for buttons when the market is up; and a few dwindling sales of scrap metal left over from World War II. A limited tourist industry also brings in a little money not counted in export totals. For years, depending largely on the price of copra and the market for trochus, exports have run between $2 and $3 million. In 1972, for example, they were $2,363,735.

In the same year, imports were reported at $26,334,062, more than ten times exports. In issuing the figure, however, the Trust Territory noted serious under-reporting of imports and estimated total imports for the year at more than *thirty million dollars*. Reported imports of beer and booze alone ran well over the total export of copra, Micronesia's only real crop. It spent about as much on rice as on booze; only two categories, building materials and clothing and textiles, came in above the pleasures of the bottle.

Inflation obviously is a factor in this precipitate climb, though inflation has not done much for the export figures. Another factor is Micronesia's soaring population, which in the long run may turn into its greatest problem. One of the fastest growing populations in the world, it is variously estimated to be gaining 3.5 to 5 percent a year and probably has doubled since 1960.

But at the moment, the most important point is that Micronesian expectations are rising even more rapidly than the population. People who once drank *tuba* now want beer, and they want it cold. And this is not just a matter of richer tastes. The population figure that is even more important than growth is that of transfer, people moving from the outer islands to the administrative centers (which pass for Micronesian cities) of Micronesia's seven districts. For example, Majuro Atoll, district center of the Marshall Islands, has gone from 5,000 to 10,000 population in the last few years and is expected to double again by 1980.

The point is that Micronesia's organized production is

very small. It falls far short of meeting its own needs even for food—let alone fiber, fuel, building materials. Only in a pure subsistence state on the outer islands, where men are in balance with the fish and with the coconuts, is the living easy. As people pour into the district centers, they necessarily turn to imported foods and materials, as well as imported pleasures.

In learning to spend the huge sums the United States has inserted unilaterally into their economy, people have developed expensive tastes—for cars and air conditioning and gold-washed Cross pens. And because the funding simply has appeared, without any real relation to their lives, they have little understanding of how a society produces wealth or of the meaning of capital accumulation.

As people come to the district centers, they come hoping for a government job—if not for themselves, then for their newly half-educated children. For here government is not the employer of last resort, but of first resort. Because of attitudes inherent in a small island subsistence-culture, working in business—that is, for another man—is considered demeaning, while working for government is seen as prestigious.

The salary scale reinforces this attitude. Government salaries are pegged at U.S. levels for fairness vis-à-vis American expatriate employees instead of at levels consistent with the Micronesian economy. This, linked with the ever greater power that a growing government asserts in a society moving rapidly to a money economy, is creating a new elite of government service which (admittedly in conjunction with other factors) is eroding the power of traditional leaders. The amazing fact is that the government employs more than half of all the salaried workers in Micronesia—and almost all of the others are doing marginal work for marginal pay and hoping, as the realization of a dream, that they too may move into the sanctified and profitable ranks of government employment.

Thus the people have come to see the government as the key to success, and education as the key to government. So they and their leaders (who by the nature of Micronesian society in fact are followers) put great pressure on educators to push every child through the schools. Family pressure on children to move from elementary to high school to college is immense, and, given the fact that the child now has almost no chance of ultimate success, probably traumatic.

There was no long-term education until the Americans arrived, so no one in Micronesia objected or perhaps even recognized that the education system was a pointless academic model that produced a half-hearted student literally prepared for nothing. Rather they noticed that from the beginning government was the only real activity the newcomers brought, and that Americans successful in government inevitably were educated. They noticed that Micronesians who prospered under the Americans were those with some English, a sense for how western society worked, and at least a little formal education. Micronesians are canny and the lesson did not have to be shouted. Their observations were confirmed when the great growth surge began in 1962, for then every Micronesian with a smattering of education found a government job awaiting him. In the next ten years government employment tripled and the future seemed unlimited. To a people who have very little way of evaluating the new society, it appeared that the key to a wealthy future was for the children to graduate from high school at least, go to work for the government, and support their parents.

Gradually the feeling arose that sharing in the new prosperity was less a matter of opportunity than of right. The feeling grew partly from the egalitarian nature of island life with its interdependent family structure in which everyone shares as a matter of right. But it arose also from the fact that the democratic concept has come to the islands casually, carelessly, its privileges and rights and opportunities much more clearly understood than its responsibilities. The result is that people there perceive democracy much more in terms of getting than of giving.

Now the unreality of the situation is catching up. Government jobs are filled with young people who are decades from retirement, and every year a new crop of youngsters, half-educated to the new society, emerges to seek jobs that are more and more scarce. To prepare themselves they have left the home islands (as more than half the elementary graduates do) and come to the district centers to high schools that continue the inadequate education they began in the island elementary schools. They reach the high school with poor preparation and finish it with skills estimated at from fifth- to seventh-grade level in a standard western academic model. And if that education is not enough to give them success in the new society, it is ample to sever them from the old subsistence-society. Not only does the lore of coconut now seem beneath them, but they have been at school during the time in their lives when critical skills of approaching adulthood are polished on the faraway island. Thus they are left as people without place or roots, and in a phrase heard more and more often in Micronesia, they "just hang around the district center." There is no work that they are willing to do, none that is commensurate with their image of themselves or paying the salaries to which they feel entitled. Because the money that poured into Micronesia never was channeled seriously into building the economy, there are few private jobs and few indeed that pay well. Furthermore, private employment, like government employment, cannot hope to keep up with the ever larger graduating classes pouring from the high schools each spring.

Waiting there in the district centers for something—anything—to happen, they are unhappy people. They loaf and drink. Alcoholism has become widely recognized as a new and dangerous social problem. Young Micronesians drink to get drunk—for release rather than conviviality—

and when liquor unlocks them, they often are dangerous.

Drunkenness is widely accepted in Micronesia as an excuse for otherwise unacceptable behavior, and young men pass abruptly from quiet drinkers to belligerent drunks. After a night of drinking, after other people have gone to bed, fights of startling violence break out and rage through the hot, dark streets. Often they begin with fists and move on to weapons. More and more frequently they end in serious injury or death. Assault is becoming a common charge. Robbery, as an expression of violence or in search of beer money, appears more and more frequently. So does suicide, a violence to the self that was almost unknown in the old society; it is an ailment of the young that shatters the old. Even rape appears, a startlingly aggressive new feature of life in a society famous for its easy sexual attitudes.

But the dissatisfaction seems to extend even to the fortunate few who land government jobs, as if they sense little real relationship between the work done and the salary paid. A different, more western kind of alcoholism, quiet and conducted at home but perhaps more deadly in the long run, and certainly indicative of a troubled society, is endemic among government employees. And indeed, the work of government in Micronesia often is obscure and equivocal, fostering as it does an ever increasing state of unreality. It is no wonder that even its employees—and certainly the people as a whole—seem to see themselves as not being in control of their lives. "They are," as Francis Hezel put it, "like coconuts on a stormy sea."

Now the living is no longer so easy. People clustered in the citylike district centers are cut off from the subsistence of their islands. Despite the foreign money that has poured in, malnutrition is becoming common in a land that has been conditioned for centuries by ample food. In the district centers, infants with kwashiorkor appear in the hospitals.

So Micronesia is on a collision course with the future. Logic says the situation must change, simply because it is growing ever less supportable. The disruptive insertion of American money has leveled out, and though it probably will continue indefinitely, any rises will simply keep up with inflation. As Micronesians cast about for a viable political future, they will have to make do with no more than they receive now, just enough to shatter the old ways but not enough to support the new. The population continues to soar, the shift to a money economy daily becomes more complete, and against all reason, expectations continue to rise. Perhaps there just are no thinkable alternatives. Blindly, obliviously, the schools graduate ever larger classes, yielding to the people's incoherent hope that education, once seen as the key to the future, can yet save the situation. Cultural dislocation increases without any recompense, and disillusionment and fear and finally anger grow. Intelligent people everywhere say that Micronesia must develop its own resources. They also say, in effect, that it has no resources.

★ ★ **CHAPTER TWO**
★

THE TINY ISLANDS AND
THEIR PEOPLE

Micronesia is dominated by the ocean. On the map the land appears as pinpricks on a field of blue. Even the shallow water in lagoons ranges to 600 feet in depth, while most of the western Pacific goes to depths of 18,000 feet; and great sections, including the vast Mariana Trench, fall into black depths below the 18,000-foot mark. The sea is always present, in the eye and in the mind, inhibiting, limiting, finally imprisoning.

This is important, because terrain and the cultural realities terrain imposes are central to understanding the social malaise which now afflicts Micronesia.

Day and night the surf breaks, thrusting at the strands of sand that protect the island proper, and the beaches always seem new drawn. Tide water flows into the lagoons clean and clear, working over the white sandy bottoms, rushing among rock and coral and barnacle clusters, inherently refreshing despite the heat of the day. As I waited on a spit of land in Palau for a ferry across the channel between Koror and Babelthuap, I watched a man with a mask, snorkel, and spear step off a jetty and drift face down in the water for a mile with hardly a motion. The air was damp and heavy, saturated: one even breathed water. An oil tank stood in the distance, an ancient landing craft—an LCVP, I think—was collapsed, half-buried in sand, on the nearby shore, and suddenly my memory ticked. I had been here before. Sometime during World War II, when I sailed with a million other men through these islands, I had stood on this spit of land and looked across this lagoon. The open water, the coral heads, the water tinting green as the eye moved, the crabs on the sandy bottom, the island green and low, another island or another point of land across the lagoon, all shimmered and blazed in the sun, real and yet also a dream. The log I kept those years ago is gone. Was I here? Perhaps—or perhaps I was having a class memory, a group recollection, of all those islands and the sun and the cool, bright, clear water greening slowly into blue, water that dominated and encompassed the land and made it, finally, a precious refuge from the motion and the iron of the ships. I believe that in the eyes of its people, it still is a refuge against the sea.

On Saipan I met Senator Petrus Tun of Yap for dinner, and after a drink he said there was a restaurant nearby named "Awesome View." Making conversation, I ventured the remark that it was aptly named, for surely the view across the great lagoon at dusk was awesome. Tun glanced at me with an odd expression. "You're in Micronesia," he said, "and everywhere you look is awesome view. Cross the island and you'll see another awesome view." That was certainly true, though I thought him rather aggressively chauvinistic. When we reached the restaurant there was a sign in front—"Ocean View." Everywhere you look in Micronesia is ocean view. Land is the anomaly here, the pinpricks like oases in a desert.

Nor does this conflict with the anthropological view that

some of the island cultures developed in interaction with each other via deep-sea sailing canoes which still operate; the perils of these extraordinary voyages over hundreds of miles of open ocean emphasize my point, as does the lack of common language among the islands. At Ponape two sailors from Kapingamarangi took me to sea on a thirty-foot double-ended canoe that had been carved from the deep red heartwood of a single giant breadfruit log. Kapingamarangi is the southernmost atoll in Micronesia, just off the equator; a considerable colony of Kapingamarangins lives on the high island of Ponape. The vessel was about two feet deep and a bare eighteen inches wide at its center, with broad gunwales on which a barefoot man could walk. Heavy breadfruit crossbars fixed an outrigger to one side and planking between the bars made a platform on the outrigger. The sail was a triangle of canvas (once pandanus-mat sails were used but they are hard to dry when soaked in a storm, and in practical Micronesia no one would dream of retaining an inconvenience for old time's sake). The sail was attached to two spars which were linked at one end to form a V.

As Deruit slipped the craft in the water, Timat walked into the forest with a machete-like saw and returned in a couple of minutes with a bamboo log twenty feet long and four inches thick. In a moment this became the mast, to which the upper spar was attached. The other end—the V-end—notched into the bow. A single line ran from the top of the mast to the outrigger. The wind filled the sail, which tautened the line to the outrigger, and Timat drew in the sheet attached to the bottom spar. Deruit gestured me onto the outrigger platform for balance, and the craft leaped ahead, everything suddenly taut and humming. This is a stone-age design, worked out in its every detail countless centuries before Europeans reached these waters, and in its application of available materials to need, it is perfect.

We were in a small bay in the lagoon, and in a hundred yards we had to come about. Timat slacked the sail, and

Deruit lifted the V of the spars from the bow and walked it aft, reversing the sail, and notched it into what had been the stern. Suddenly stern became bow and bow stern, and still the outrigger was to windward and the single line to the mast was taut. Now Timat moved abaft the mast, drew in the sheet, and the canoe tacked off in a new direction, running up the wind. Now and then Timat dipped a slender, pointed paddle into the sea as a rudder, but most of his steering was done with the sail itself. For one who had matured in an era fascinated by machines, the combination of simplicity and efficiency was stunning.

Soon we came to the coral reef that guards the lagoon. Timat was slightly out of the channel, and the water greened suddenly. Coral heads, white and ghostly, came up beneath us, and the canoe bumped and bucked for a moment, gouging the hard coconut-wood strip laid along the keel for protection. Deruit laughed and Timat looked discomfited and then the canoe bumped free and took the rolling swells of the Pacific and I forgot the men. The slender canoe was buoyant as a cork, swift as a knife. It sliced up the face of the swell, topped it with the pointed bow sharp against the sky, shipped water and spray that glittered in the sun, and swept down into the new trough. Only a few inches above the water it all was loud and immediate, the hiss of the hull in the water, the spray, the wind in the sail, the hull recording each tremor of the moving water and passing it into your body and mind. These boats become one with the sea and even today men take them a thousand miles and more without instruments, navigating by signs, watermarks, and the actual shape, direction, and texture of the waves themselves in a manner too mystic and complex for western technological man to grasp readily, but bringing them to land fall when their target is an island only a half-mile wide, standing no taller than a palm, and when the waves are high as the mast of the canoe. When storms come they lower the sail and wait; and if it is very bad they turn the canoe over and cling to its gunwales, breathing the air trapped inside. For centuries they have traveled thus. Some are lost in the great storms, and some are blown so far off course they never return. Kapingamarangi itself was settled by a Polynesian strain unlike other Micronesian peoples that is believed to have ridden a great canoe in on a storm centuries ago. Micronesia is a land and a people dominated by distance and the sea, their tiny islands refuges from the deluge.

At 1:00 P.M. on January 7, 1958, a typhoon struck the atoll of Jaluit in the Marshall Islands. Typhoons are circular storms that strike and move around and strike again. Over nine-and-a-half hours this storm struck the several islands of Jaluit three times, and the last was much the worst. The Jaluit radio first reported the storm to the district center 147 miles away at Majuro at 3:15 P.M. and fell silent. At 5:30 P.M. it reported swells of green water three to four feet deep, sweeping clear over the island from both the sea side and the lagoon side. Then there were no further transmissions. Coconut trees sixty to ninety feet tall were uprooted and jumbled in log piles. Flying sticks speared people as they ran, and sheet-metal roofing flew like knives. People hid in concrete cisterns and crawled among the tangled coconut logs for protection. The third strike came after dark with winds estimated at 135 mph, and most of the last buildings and the strongest trees went down. The casualty count was not precise; one account lists eight killed and sixteen missing and presumed swept out to sea. But a sense of the damage can be found in the stark report of a Trust Territory official named Boyd Mackenzie, who went to Jaluit as soon as the water calmed. In his *Paradise in Trust*, Robert Trumbull quoted Mackenzie:

Many of the islands were swept clear of all trees and houses . . . coconut trees 80 per cent destroyed . . . all coconuts knocked down including flowers . . . all

subsistence plants destroyed by wind and salt water
. . . all houses not built of concrete destroyed . . .
water cisterns on all islands but Jabor not potable . . .
most of the foodstuffs . . . destroyed or swept out to
sea . . . most of the people's belongings lost . . . all
but two small lagoon sailboats destroyed . . . many
canoes destroyed.

[Of Kili] The area was swept clean by the storm and
nothing recovered . . . the cargo pier has been completely smashed . . . it is just a mass of rocks that
have been thrown into a huge pile . . .

[Of Imiej] The south end where there were five acres
of coconut palms was completely swept off the island,
leaving nothing but hard coral and loose rocks. The
entire frontage on the ocean side has been completely
denuded of all foilage and trees (little over three-
quarters of the island).

[Of Aroen] All coconut and breadfruit trees had
been knocked down and water damage covered the
entire island . . .

Majeto Island was one of the worst seen. The entire
island was devastated by the high waves which swept
across it . . . The erosion is very bad . . . with complete loss of two to three feet of top soil which has
been swept into the sea. Coconut trees, pandanus, and
large breadfruit trees were swept into the lagoon at
least a hundred yards from the present shoreline. All
the houses and cisterns were completely destroyed and
swept into the lagoon.

It will be at least six months before any work can be
done on these islands, as in the spring tide water will
run across the entire island [because the barrier
strands had been washed away].

The two small islands across from Boklaplap have
been fused into one island, swept clean of all vegetation . . . Jebet . . . has been almost completely destroyed, leaving about one acre of land, all trees and

foliage have been leveled. Jar . . . has lost about two acres of land with all trees down.*

The Pacific presses these points of land which are mountaintops that rise from a vast sea bottom and barely scratch the surface. The word Micronesia can be translated as "tiny islands." Of more than 2,100, only 94 are usually inhabited, though turtling parties sometimes visit others. The borders of such a domain obviously are fluid, but it is said to cover three million square miles of ocean and sometimes is described as one of the seven largest politically united areas in the world. Geographically, Micronesia includes more than the Trust Territory of the Pacific Islands. It includes the American territory of Guam (the largest Micronesian island with 216 square miles), the tiny independent republic of Nauru, and the Gilbert Islands, which the British still hold. In common usage, however, Micronesia and the Trust Territory are interchangeable, the first applying to the terrain and to the people, and the second to the government structure.

Thus, excluding Guam, the Trust Territory has in those three million watery square miles exactly 707.442 square miles of land area, according to a satellite-mapping project completed in 1973. A few islands are fair sized. Ponape has 127 square miles, for example, and Saipan has 47. But Majuro in the Marshalls is 30 miles long and rarely more than 400 yards wide, and there is no place that one cannot see ocean in both directions.

High islands generally are volcanic mountain peaks around which the sea has built a reef of living, ever growing organisms, to trap a lagoon of quiet water. The highest, Agrihan, is 3,166 feet. Low islands (the highest point in the Marshalls, for example, is thirty-three feet) are coral reefs which probably once surrounded high islands that sank

* Robert Trumbull, *Paradise in Trust: A Report on Americans in Micronesia 1946–1951*, (New York: Sloane, 1959), pp. 26–32.

over millions of years. As the mountain sank into the lagoon, the coral collar of the reef continued to grow, since it lives precisely at the oxygenated surface of the sea. Gradually the reef collected sand in which seeds were placed by birds and waves, vegetation appeared, soil collected, and over a million years there appeared a new island to which life could cling. The result was several islands linked by the reef around the lagoon, which is considered part of the living space. Kwajalein, where the United States maintains a missile base, is the largest atoll in the world with more than one thousand square miles of lagoon. Truk is apparently a combination, a cluster of high islands which probably are the eroded peaks of a single great mountain, with barrier reefs forming a huge lagoon that once served as a major Japanese fleet anchorage.

Three archipelagoes combine to form Micronesia. The Marianas Islands (which include Guam) lie to the north. The Marshall Islands lie farthest to the east, almost 2,300 miles from Hawaii. The Caroline Islands sprawl westward across the ocean from the Marshalls and south of the Marianas. The Marianas and Marshalls each form an administrative district of the Trust Territory. The Eastern Carolines include Ponape District, just to the west, and Truk District (another district, Kusaie, is separating from Ponape District). The Western Carolines include Yap District and, on the westernmost end, Palau District, the outermost island of which is a bare two hundred miles from New Guinea.

The district centers are served by jet aircraft operating on fairly reliable twice weekly schedules, but the outer islands are reached slowly by small field-trip ships. A ship is expected to call at each island every six weeks, but the ships often break down and are buffered by weather, so no islander can count on a schedule. One reason that Kusaie wanted to separate from Ponape, in addition to its speaking a different language, is that it lies 347 miles from Ponape and its 3,989 people grew tired of waiting endlessly for the field-trip ship. As a separate district, it probably can command air service. That is hardly a record distance, though; the farthest school which the education director at Yap must supervise is on Lamotrek Atoll, 583 open sea miles away; and in the Marshalls, Eniwetok is 683 miles from the district center at Majuro.

Most of the outer islands have radios, though a combination of salt air and the technical inexperience of island people usually defeats machines. An important election fell while I was on Ponape. A close race on Ponape Island depended on the box at Pingelap Atoll (they gerrymander in Micronesia, too) but the Pingelap radio was out. The election results would have to await the field-trip ship's call at Pingelap, but unfortunately, the ship was broken down at Nukuro Atoll (with the district director of education aboard) and no one knew when it would be fixed.

On Census Day, September 18, 1973, the Trust Territory had 112,649 people, of whom 56 percent were 21 or younger, another sign of startling population growth. There were also 4,168 expatriates, most of them Americans.

The district with the largest land area was Ponape before Kusaie split off with 186.505 square miles of land, on which 23,118 people live. The Marianas, which include Saipan, the Trust Territory capital, and 181.869 square miles and 13,081 people. Palau had 177.599 square miles and 12,782 people. The Marshalls total only 69.286 miles and have 24,299 people. Yap has 46.810 square miles and a population of 7,747. Truk is the smallest in area with 45.373 square miles, and the largest in population with 31,441, which bears on why the social malaise now overtaking Micronesia is most advanced there. There were 181 people at sea on Census Day.

Micronesians are combinations of various ethnic types from around the Pacific basin, generally brown-skinned with coarse black hair and a tendency toward thickness of body, limb, and features. They speak at least nine mutually unintelligible languages, and they certainly require outside pressure to see themselves as Micronesians. Nationhood is

still a distant concept even for the most politically sophisticated. A man sees himself as of Jaluit, and then of the
Marshalls, and hardly at all of Micronesia.

Yet I will generalize about them and their culture, for
their differences are not germane to my subject, which is
the part the United States has played in the social malaise
gripping them all. They are immensely complicated people
whom anthropologists spend lifetimes studying, only to
wonder at the end how much they really have learned. Recognizing that complexity, I will try to deal only with the
parts of Micronesian culture that seem to exacerbate the
malaise—for understanding that exacerbation is critical to
understanding the malaise itself. The views that follow are
anthropologically sound, but they are based on my own observation and interviews.

I believe that the key cultural point in today's dilemma is
the pressure of life on a small island on the individual and
on the community.

Micronesians are reserved and rarely explain themselves.
Their thought patterns seem more oriented to the east than
to the west. Their solutions to problems, including problems related to western technology, are pragmatic and related to their own environment. Perhaps as a result of this,
some visitors tend to see them as a childlike, quaint people
and to tell funny anecdotes about them. I must say that I
found them to be tough, resilient, and intelligent. They are
politically adept—perhaps because living in harmony on a
tiny island amounts to a political act—and in their continuing negotiations with the United States on their political
status in the future, they have proven themselves sophisticated and capable despite their limited background.

Some things about their attitudes simply are inexplicable
to the outsider. A certain village in Yap, for example, considered a particular offshore reef its communal property.
The reef was rich in sea turtles, which are good to eat and
have symbolic significance there. Visitors sometimes captured and ate the turtles, which was acceptable, but when

the village learned that a man from an adjoining village (inter-village feeling can be brutal) who was guiding visitors also was eating the turtle meat, it was enraged. Word was passed commanding the man not to eat another bite of turtle, and when he disobeyed these private orders a party from the injured village dragged him from his house and beat him. The story generally is true—my source saw the man in the hospital at Colonia, the district center at Yap— but I do not think the situation is to be considered in western terms.

District centers simulate small towns today, but the Micronesian heritage is rural. Of course, the smallness of the island is relative. Fewer than a hundred people may live on an atoll, while several thousand may live on a larger island. But there the society tends to break down into communal villages that are nearly as isolated and territory-conscious as are atoll communities. I believe that in the terms of my consideration the differences between the two are slight.

Subsistence society in a relatively pure state, which holds on many Micronesian islands even today, was theoretically ideal. The only real dangers lay in storms and, ironically, in drought on some atoll islands where the rainfall varied wildly and there was almost no water storage capacity in the sandy soil. Otherwise there were not many problems. Food was usually plentiful—coconuts, taro (a nutritious rootstock vegetable not dissimilar to the sweet potato), breadfruit, huge Pacific yams, mangoes, pandanus, and other fruits and vegetables. The reef provided ample fish and shellfish. It was a balanced system—everyone worked, everyone ate. Shelter was simple and warmth was never a problem. Unlike other societies in which people had to struggle for existence, here the living generally was easy.

Work was essential and sometimes hard and occasionally, as when the sea was running, dangerous. But it was never constant nor did it ever demand labor from dawn to dusk. Rather it was done as needed, often on impulse, often in groups as in fishing or digging taro, so that it had a social and even a sporting note. There was ample time for doing as one pleased, which in the humid tropics often meant resting. It was not a life to implant a burning work ethic or to make western work patterns attractive. That is one reason that the work habits expected in an Americanized society are not warmly received in Micronesia.

The islands were self-sustaining, even after the copra trade began to bring in western implements, and many remain so today. Thus it was a balanced system which depended on a balanced society which was static by nature. Success depended on using the resources well and fully. As techniques for doing so were perfected, they became ritualized. (As a result, when innovation appeared, with its capacity for upsetting balances, it was perceived as threatening.) Wisdom related to experience and to following immutable laws, not to ideas and to imagination. Youngsters were expected to honor and to emulate their elders and were not considered worth hearing until they were forty or so. Dirty jobs were reserved for the young, who thus learned and at the same time moved to full membership in the society—a membership earned by mastery of things known and of things past, not of things new.

It is hard to imagine a life less consistent with competitive, individualized modern education with its focus on grades, personal achievement, and the grasp of new ideas.

Since nothing was expected to change, there was little reason for planning, and even today Micronesians seem to give little consideration to the future. Sooner or later the fish will run and then the men will catch them. This may be why there is little broad interest in the political future. A spokesman for the Trust Territory's Education-for-Self-Government program called on a small island and said the only question asked him was, "How much rice did the ship bring?" A naval officer in gold braid visited an island, talked at length, and asked for questions. Finally the senior chief said, "May I have your hat?" Sometimes such stories are told to indicate Micronesian innocence, but I think they illustrate a conceptual grasp of life. It is a concept at odds, of course, with the modern society now coming down upon them.

This attitude also relates to why there is so little institutionalization all across the Pacific. Relationships tend to be personal and to rely on oral contact. Even among literate Micronesians, for example, letters count for little and often are not answered, nor is what they say accepted—let alone integrated—into an ongoing situation. Norman Meller, a political scientist at the University of Hawaii who helped guide the Congress of Micronesia into existence, is particularly aware of this. "Well, for instance, one of the key differences between American administrators and Micronesians is that the American tends to deal in formalized ways, with emphasis on written materials. He doesn't feel something is settled until it's written down. And he's time-conscious, schedule-oriented. Most Pacific Islanders aren't time conscious. The more westernized they become, the more conscious of time they get—you can see the change. There's a whole series of nuances, but my point is that there is no institutionalized follow-through, no way to set some thing in motion and expect it to follow an orderly, agreed upon, scheduled path. And this frustrates lots of Americans."

"Micronesian time" is a phrase Americans throughout the islands use constantly, at first in despair and later in comfort, since it also relieves them of the necessity for promptness. It means simply that things will be done when the doer gets around to it. "Assume," a well educated Micronesian said to me, "that there's to be a party at six, and the ones bringing the pig or the yam or the beer don't arrive until eight. What does it matter? We know they are coming. The important point is not the time of the act but the quality of the act." It was useless to suggest, of course, that time is key to the certainty of an act—a discipline of performance—for this holds only in a large society. On a small island there is no escaping the duty or the expectation of others.

American students of Micronesia believe that the western cause-and-effect approach is inconsistent with Micronesian thinking, which is based on a much wider frame, including magic and various spiritual factors. Some people describe Micronesian thinking as "circular" (as opposed to western linear thinking), and there is no doubt that the Micronesian approach is fundamentally indirect. Much Micronesian thought is allegorical, as in the idea that to hit is to miss, to miss is to hit. David Ramarui, an interesting, reflective man who is Director of Education for the Trust Territory government, describes a Palauan needle fish whose mouth is so far back on his body that he must pass his prey to strike it: to pass or miss it is to hit it, to hit it directly is to miss it. The same point is true in dealings among humans, which accounts for the pained silence that often occurs when an American asks a direct question. Newly arrived Americans make suggestions for direct and logical action that they feel will solve the problem at hand immediately. They receive smiles, silence, gracious murmurs, which they take for acquiescence. They assume the solution is accepted and the matter resolved. It really is too easy to deal out here, they write home. In a few months they find nothing is solved, the response had no real meaning other than form, and it really is too hard to deal out here.

Such an island life, which may seem idyllic at first glance, probably is costly in human terms, both in psychic pressures and in limitations. Dr. William Vitarelli, an educator and an interesting man who has been a gadfly stinging the Trust Territory administration for more than two decades, remembers going to a little island for the first time. "I was new out here then, and I remember we ran up the lagoon for forty miles or so, to a little island at the end of the atoll, and it was magnificent and the life seemed perfectly balanced. They welcomed us and built a fire there on the beach and the kids went out in the lagoon and started splashing the water and pretty soon they threw up a lot of fish on the beach and these went right into the fire. Kids brought fresh limes and a couple of oranges, the fish were done and put on a big pandanus mat and out of the coals came bread-fruit—just like sweet potatoes—and it was marvelous. You ate the fish whole, you could avoid the guts easily and peel the skin off, and finally we were done and everyone sat around under the trees. But what then? I began talking to the kids—I had some candy and of course they loved candy—but after we'd talked about fish and coconuts we had exhausted the conversation. And I began to wonder, what kind of a life is this? And I have to believe that idyllic as you may make life on these islands, they offer very little. An amoeba is balanced too, after all."

The fact seems to be that life on an island a half-mile square with a hundred-odd people, where ideas are foreign and antithetical, and the ruling forces are a combination of magic and physical facts is basically boring. When children's minds have been opened, first by the island school and then by advanced school in the district center, naturally it is difficult to get them to go home—and more difficult to keep them there.

It is obvious that such a society depended on consensus. One simply could not live one's life on a small island with enemies; the alternatives would be to get along or to kill. The containment of the island compressed by the surrounding sea and the inability to leave even for a moment made intense pressure. Many observers feel that the capacity to express anger within their own group was almost bred out of these people because such expression was too dangerous to the existence of a stabilized, static society. But of course, people pay a penalty—if psychic and hidden—for such necessities.

Another force for balance of consensus was the emphasis on the communal. There was little to mark the individual. People dressed alike and lived in similar houses. Individual competitiveness was acceptable in achievements such as catching more fish, but it was foreign and unacceptable in terms of amassing possessions, and attempts to do so were deeply resented and usually were punished. The society was equal and it meant to stay that way. (Even today in some parts of Micronesia, and particularly in tradition-bound Yap, businessmen who have the acumen to rise above their fellows are at pains to show by dress and living style that they do not see themselves as newly superior.) The result was an individually non-competitive society, which of course is quite at odds with the nature of the society now coming to Micronesia. What wealth could be amassed (indigenous money of shell and stone in Palau and Yap, food everywhere) was massed society-wide, throughout one island or the village.

The vent for man's competitiveness was between these social groups. Francis Hezel of Truk tells of shaming feasts: one village invites another to a feast; if the inviting (challenging) village provides more food than the other village members can eat, it wins and shames the invitees; but if *they* can eat all that is available and look around in simulated hunger for more, they win.

Leaders faced this same problem. This is a society in which leaders govern by the consent of the governed. The leadership structure on the islands was and still is most complex, and few Americans understand it. Clearly, however, leaders were very conscious of maintaining their support. They lived and worked generally as did everyone else. They did not put on many airs; status was accorded rather than taken. Status was achieved occasionally by prowess but more generally by carefully evolved caste positions. Since these positions were held by the consent of the people, the leaders in effect did not rule but mediated.

Americans often are frustrated at island councils or gatherings of clan leaders. Each leader sits apart from others with messengers at his call. At some point he sends a messenger to whisper to another leader. No one knows what was said, or if it was of substance. Most important, no public commitment has been made. John Dorrance, an American foreign service officer who has sat through more such meetings than he cares to remember, notes that messages move back and forth, hours drag by, and visiting Americans sit baffled. Finally a senior leader offers the decision. Americans often asssume that he has at last spoken what he could have spoken at the start—he is, as they see it, the leader, after all—but in fact the whole process appears designed to achieve a consensus which the chief has simply announced.

This secretiveness, however, permeates the culture and again relates to the pressure which an island imposes on its people. No one lets others know exactly what he is thinking or how he really feels. Face is all important and no man, high or low, may be contradicted or denied. As a correlation, of course, no man puts himself in a position to allow this to happen. When the Palau Legislature was formed, it was named the *Olbiil era Kelulau*, which can be translated in various ways: one is "place where important things are discussed quietly," while Meller translates it as "meeting place of whispers," and Father Felix Yoach, president of the Micronesian board of education and one of two Micronesian priests (both Jesuits), as "words of wisdom—but whispered."

This caution and consensus within the group may account for the harsh prejudices Micronesians show toward people from different islands (or on slightly larger islands from different villages). Anger must be vented somewhere. Puluwatans sailed not so long ago to Pulusuk, an island to which they felt they had proprietary rights based on ancient war actions, and, like pirates of old, threatened the inhabitants with knives.* On Yap, when children from two villages were sent to a single school, they readily obeyed

* Thomas Gladwin, *East Is a Big Bird* (Cambridge: Harvard University Press, 1970), pp. 16–17.

teachers from their own village but were unmanageable
with teachers from the other village. Eventually they had to
be separated. Micronesians discriminate shamefully against
outer islanders. Most district centers have ghettos to which
outer islanders are consigned, like the Kapingamarangi village on Ponape where Deruit and Timat live.

Human anger runs in these people too, but it must be
submerged beyond self-recognition in dealing with their
own community if the community is to survive. This act of
burying emotion deep in the psyche must be extremely
powerful. And the resulting attitudes conflict immediately
with work in a modern western society. It is hard for such
people to give or to accept orders. It is hard to demand specific performance at a specific time or to evaluate another
person or to punish failure or to fire someone. Micronesians
strenuously avoid such actions, which is one reason government is so huge; people are transferred, not fired.

When elections (an American import) are contested without a clear community position developing, voter turnout
often is low because people would rather not vote than vote
against someone. And Micronsian elections seem to be decided less on issues than on family or clan connections. I
was there during the election of delegates to the constitutional convention, and I did not hear a word about what
sort of future various candidates envisioned. It appeared
solely a matter of connections.

Political campaigning becomes a different art on a small
island where everyone knows you. Having had some experience in American politics, I described a campaign for the
U.S. Senate to Petrus Tun, the senator for Yap, and asked
how he campaigned. Tun is an engaging, experienced man
now in his late thirties who has traveled widely; on one
trip, for example, he spent several months in New York at
the United Nations and then went on to Rotterdam where
his wife was finishing an eight-month course in nutrition.
"Well," he said, "everyone on the island knows you or
knows who you are. And you can't tell them what you've

done because that would be to put yourself forward, that would be—what?—unseemly. So you have your friends go about telling the great things you've done. And you follow them, telling that they exaggerate, that really it was not so much. And this is the point: you must be very clever in saying that what you've done is not so important while conveying the idea that in fact it was important. Now, the people already know who you are and what you've done and what they think of it; and when you speak, they know what you are doing and why; their interest lies in how well you do it. To be able to make a modest statement that one is not important persuade that in fact one is important is the key and sometimes, well, that can be difficult. But that is what interests them. And then, of course, too, if you have an opponent you must find ways to put him off balance so that he will say more or less directly what he wants and of course no one will like that and then you will win. That is politics in Micronesia." He might have added, however, that his prominent family didn't hurt, either.

Part of the pressure of living on a small island comes from the literal shortage of land. For Micronesians, as Dorrance puts it, "the smaller the island, the more important the land. There is a mystical attachment that goes far beyond an individual. Land belongs to a lineage, to the dead, the living, the yet unborn." This is the reason that for most Micronesians, the sale of land is unthinkable. This also leads to the fear that surrounds the issue and the power that the community can exercise on the individual. As man depends generally on land for life, he does so immediately in a subsistence society, and in Micronesia the land is taken. On a small island, there is that much and no more; on a large island, each clan will defend its territory. So banishment from the community can be the equivalent of death. This feeling looms very large in the Micronesian mind, and I think it is realistic. This is the discipline that the chief—presumably acting for the community—can and will exert on those who challenge the consensus. Every island seems to have a symbolic term for banishment. Father Yoach, in Palau, noting that the very act of political campaigning or even of voting, in places where the chief perceives it as a threat to the community's integrity, could result in an individual being disciplined, used the phrase "cut his pole"— that is, cut a pole for a man to use to pole his canoe away, to leave the island, the community. On another island the term is "to give him a canoe," and on another "to build his raft." Sometimes a small model of a canoe or of a raft is placed before a man's house, a far more deadly symbol than a fiery cross, for on the compressed island there is nowhere to go.

Thus conformity is not just a matter of following the imperatives of the situation but can be enforced. The need for conformity and the consensus approach is burned deeply in the Micronesian nature and character. It is little wonder that he is somewhat disoriented when thrust into a modern society which demands individual thought and action and puts its highest premium on individual achievement, or that western education, with its stress on individual competition for grades and acts of initiative, should tend to sever the child from his past.

Finally, however, it seems clear that life in Micronesia provided a high level of security. It was a comfortable society if one did not challenge it: plenty to eat, ample shelter and warmth, not a great deal of work, few external dangers. Everyone knew everyone and internal conflict was buried. Occasional inter-clan or inter-village wars apparently were more ritualistic than real. The significance of Tun's description of campaigning is that it admitted nothing that was new and thus threatening.

Further security lies in the extended family, which is widely recognized as a key problem today as the society seeks to change from old to new. In a communal society in which there was no ownership and the individual was subordinated, the family structure became correspondingly more important. Relationships were carefully tabulated, even unto the tenth cousin and beyond. And since all owned and none owned, all shared; thus no one could go hungry, for if one had, all had. It did little to fit people for a new society based on individual accomplishment; but so long as the subsistence island society held, the extended family meant the sharing and thus the lowering of whatever risks life held—to the point that risk was almost voided and life was quite secure and comfortable. And it could stay that way so long as no new ideas and opportunities appeared. But today new ideas and opportunities are beating on Micronesia like the surf.

And the changes they will bring are certain to be conditioned by these three elemental points—that the life produced a static society ill equipped to deal with new, dynamic forms; that it demanded a high level of consensus which is at odds with the individualism demanded today; and that it produced a high sense of security that makes risk-taking less attractive.

Still, David Ramarui, the education director and a student of Micronesian culture, refuses to believe that the change will not be positive. He is from Palau, which was the most highly developed of the Japanese holdings, and he went to the famous carpentry school at Koror that was Japan's highest level of education open to Micronesians. Then came the war and everything started over. He talks very slowly, his quick mind searching out the analogies he likes, his smile warm and easy:

"In Palau, we say that change, and acculturation too, is like a tide. It comes up, and you must move or get wet. In the channel between Koror and the large island, Babelthuap, the current is swift when the tide comes up. But the tide moves out, too, and again it is swift. Progress, growth, cuts two ways, up or down, good or bad. Acculturation does not—need not—destroy culture, as we see it. We all develop new things. We apply old things to the new. The word for canoe—we use it now for car, transportation. I believe we must keep the basics of modern education, but we must include real teaching of Micronesian cultures. Not for identity—that argument for identity as such seems emotional to me—no, because our cultures carry values inherent to this kind of environment. We've got to teach English and do it well, not to take the place of Micronesian languages, but because the knowledge we need is in English repositories, the libraries, the reference material, even the newspapers that we don't have.

"There is a tool, a Palauan tool that once was made of shell sharpened on stone. It is a blade on a handle like a small axe, but the blade is turned so that it is like a small mattock, but very sharp. Now it is made in Japan, of steel. Before, all boys were given that tool, and by the time they were ten, they could use tools. It is very useful—it carves, it chops—when a boy knows that tool he knows something of his world.

"And Micronesians don't plan much. They live what is. They imitate Americans now because that is an—an available model. But they don't plan. There is a men's house [a large, wonderfully ornate structure with a high peaked roof, rich in symbolic overtones in several Micronesian cultures] on Babelthuap that was built in the old way. It probably took four or five years. People worked on it when they were ready and in the meantime the wood aged. It's about a hundred years old now and it is very sound. In Koror they built one a few years ago with modern tools and a typhoon blew it down. They built another and the wood shrunk and they had to prop it up with poles. It was not planning that made the old house sound—they followed life and the wood cured.

"My home was on Babelthuap, and when I went to the University[of Hawaii] I was away five years. My brother was nine years studying in the [mainland] U.S. and when we were finished I joined him there and we traveled over much of the country. And all that time we spoke in English, but I told my brother, 'When you come back to Palau, you will speak in Palauan.'

"There was a water shortage that year and when we returned, my brother, who had studied medical technology, could see how bad our water system was. He decided to buy a small pump and dig a well and lay out pipes and install plumbing. He drew plans, he worked it all out, and when my father saw them, he said, 'This is not necessary. We have lived all our lives here and we're still healthy.' In effect he contradicted my brother's education and my brother was sad. Several weeks later, my father had been away and he returned and was talking. We have a good concept of money in Palau in terms of value decisions. My father began talking of Palauan money [of shell] which represents value because it represents effort to cut and shape it. And my brother said, 'Why don't you take your Palauan money and throw it into the ocean—it buys nothing at the store!' My father was shocked, and I suppose hurt, and later he came to me and asked me why my brother would say such a thing. And I said, 'You live in two worlds . . .' "

★
★ ★ CHAPTER THREE
★

THE AMERICANS ARRIVE

Micronesia has been a colonial empire for 450 years and no one yet has made it a financial success, which explains some of the problem today as its people newly aspire to a place in the modern industrial world. Spain was first, after Magellan's initial landfall in the Marianas, and it held on for centuries, though it was a British skipper who slipped into the Marshall Islands and named them for himself. Spain's myopic colonial policy focused on gold and the Cross. It used Guam as a watering place for galleons running from Mexico to Manila. On the return trips the great ships swept far to the north to pick up favorable easterly winds. Since the early Spanish probed among the islands more by chance then by intent, they probably never knew the extent of the Micronesian empire they claimed.

Missionary priests brought their version of God's word and enforced it with righteous brutality. The story is not clear, but apparently the native peoples paid a heavy price for this benefit. Early missionaries estimated that 70,000 to 100,000 people lived in the Marianas alone. These people resisted the newcomers and in several vicious actions were nearly destroyed. A census taken in 1710 showed 3,672 native people while one in 1756 showed only 1,600. It is believed that the native people, unable to prevail against Spanish arms, turned to abortion, infanticide, and suicide—which may speak to the situation faced in Micronesia today. Ancient house foundations in the main islands of Yap indicate that 60,000 people may have lived there once, but only about 4,000 are there today. What happened is not known, and certainly European disease took many of them. This decimation, however, explains why the Marianas people, known today as Chomorros, are really a mixture of many peoples who have passed through and thus have less sense of heritage than do most Micronesians. And that may be part of the reason they now are severing their relations with the rest of Micronesia to tie their future to the United States. They are as rootless as we are.

Yet as the Spanish rule progressed, there appeared the ambivalence that has marked European and American incursions ever since. On the one hand, the Spanish saw the native peoples as inhuman and savage, eaters of human flesh, barbarians better dead than unredeemed. At the same time, however, there was a conflicting vision of the native peoples as children of nature living in a tropical paradise. For the Spanish, though, the matter was somewhat academic; they were willing enough for those natives who accepted the church to live otherwise untouched on their unspoiled—that is, undeveloped—islands, for the Spanish had no other interest there.

The Germans, on the other hand, arrived with quite different views. They introduced Protestantism as a consequence of their presence, but their interest was commercial. In the late nineteenth century they established themselves in the Marshalls through that favored colonial device, the trading firm, which they called the Jaluit Company (for the island on which it headquartered). When the United States took Guam after the Spanish-American War, Germany bought the rest of Micronesia, and the Spanish departed. The Protestant faith eventually overtook about one third of the people. Germany also introduced commercial agriculture for the first time and established coconut plantations, planting the trees fifteen feet apart in orderly rows; some of those towering lines are still bearing today. Out of his own interest in the subject, a German merchant prince sponsored a young anthropologist who made a multi-volume study of Micronesian culture. It remains a classic and was unequalled until the anthropological study the U.S. Navy conducted after World War II. Yet the German colony was never successful in its primary purpose of commerce, nor did many Germans actually come out to the faraway islands. And as World War I opened, the Germans lost their hold.

Japan, the third master of Micronesia, began the change that so rattles the islanders today. For Japan came with different notions and intentions and a different view of its own role. By the end of the last century, new industrialization was making Japan a power. As it considered expansion, the islands were a natural step, a warm weather adjunct spread across the sea just a bit beyond Japan's horizon. Modern Japanese tourists still view Guam as their Bermuda. When war began in Europe in 1914, Japan moved quietly into the islands and took control. The Germans packed and shipped for home.

The Japanese came to stay. A trace of that impulse can be seen today in the buildings they raised. Many still stand, for they were made of heavy concrete to withstand typhoons and years. Today they have a massive, mysterious look, their walls mildewed nearly black, some with iron shutters against narrow windows, bearing an odd, angular design that you recognize instantly as of a different culture.

The Japanese saw the islands less as a foreign colony to be exploited than as a natural extension of a new Japanese empire. Micronesia had strategic value, it served as a population outlet for the crowded home islands, it could supply food, sugar, copra, and the industrial alcohol needed at home—and it had the same south-seas lure for the Japanese that has drawn every other visitor. The Treaty of Versailles ratified the Japanese move, and in 1920 the League of Nations mandated control of all of Micronesia except Guam to Japan, and for years thereafter the islands were known informally as the Mandates.

There was a xenophobic quality to Japan's administration, and outsiders were barred. The rest of the world assumed that Japan was fortifying the islands in violation of the mandate. Deeply interested, the U.S. Navy tried various ruses to penetrate the islands, around which every game plan for war in the Pacific turned. Amelia Earhart, possibly acting as a U.S. spy, was lost in Micronesia in 1937, and there are some indications that she died in Japanese hands. But research in Japan after the war indicates that in fact serious fortification did not begin until shortly before the war and was not completed when the war began.

Instead the Japanese had treated the islands as an extension of Japan that was to be developed commercially. It used a civilian trading firm, the famed Nanyo Boeki Kaisha, Ltd., as a development vehicle and put administration into the hands of the South Seas Bureau, a civilian agency named with some sense of the Japanese feeling for the islands. And it built roads, docks, water catchments, cisterns, sea-plane ramps, and those ubiquitous concrete buildings with their thick walls and narrow windows.

Japan was not very successful at commercial development in Micronesia—so little is there to develop—but it did set in motion absolute change. In the district centers, especially in Palau and the Marianas, where the Japanese presence was heaviest, the people began the profound shift from a subsistence to a money economy. That change shook the Micronesian lifestyle to its heart and continues to shake it today, when the change is much more pervasive. That this is a change facing any subsistence economy that enters the modern world makes it no less profound.

Some of the money economy appeared as wages to pay Micronesians to work on sugar plantations, the only large-scale agriculture other than copra ever known in Micronesia, before or since. The Japanese kept livestock, raised vegetables to send back to the home islands, and mined phosphate from deposits now exhausted. By 1938 exports had risen to $11,730,000, going almost entirely to Japan, while imports were at a comfortable $7,665,000. It was a favorable balance of trade that has never occurred since.

But for comparison, it is useful to remember that today expatriates make up less than four percent of Micronesia's population. Most of the money changing hands under the Japanese, however, was changing in Japanese hands, for at this point there were more expatriates in Micronesia than there were Micronesians. Norman Meller writes that in 1940 there were 29,000 Asians living in the town of Garapan on Saipan, which was five times the number of native peoples in all the Marianas.* Pictures of Garapan at the time look rather like a modern subdivision, with rows of neat stucco houses, each with a water catchment and cistern. At about this time the islands of Palau had some 22,000 Palauans and almost 39,000 Japanese, Koreans, and Okinawans.

The Japanese welcomed Micronesians into their system, but kept them firmly on its bottom. The system was for the benefit of Japan, and the function of Micronesians was to provide its basic labor. Intermarriage was encouraged, with Japanese citizenship awarded the Micronesian so favored. The paternalistic attitude was nicely caught in a quotation which I. G. Edmonds cites from Shokichi Yamaguchi's 1927 book, *Moral Nature of Uncivilized People:*

> The Japanese people, traditionally impatient, desired the islanders to speed up their advancement, as a

* Norman Meller, *The Congress of Micronesia* (Honolulu: University of Hawaii Press), 1969, p. 11.

mother wishes to have her baby walk when it can still
only crawl. To this end the government made primary
education compulsory for native children, established
public schools and young men's associations and com-
pelled attendance at both.

The mode of living and clothing and the industrial
activity of the islanders are being transformed. A large
majority of the people, men and women, young and
old, have begun to wear clothes. Their dwellings are
now floored. . . . Roads, not jungle paths, connect the
villages. . . . Natives have new delicacies like rice,
bread, tinned foodstuffs, sugar and confec-
tionaries . . .*

The Japanese established strong schools for their own
children and rudimentary schools, generally of three grades,
for Micronesian children. They taught children to speak
Japanese, to read it at a simple level, and to calculate. A picture of the day shows a serious Japanese man with a long
stick instructing a crowded class of Micronesian youngsters
in Japanese symbols chalked on a black board. Many older
Micronesians still speak Japanese, and sometimes Japanese
tourists are amused, for the language is a servant's form.
The teachers were stern, and children were punished if they
used their native language at school.

The schools did little to expand the world view of Micronesians; rather they aimed for a student subservient to Japanese interests, who was not likely to rise beyond semi-
skilled labor and certainly was not likely to reach any
personal independence in life. Artisans and technicians
were almost entirely Japanese. A few of the most apt Micronesian students were given an extra two years of schooling, and of these a very few went on to three-year trade
schools, the best known of which was the carpentry school

* Cited by I. G. Edmonds in *Micronesia, America's Outpost in the Pacific*
(New York: Bobbs-Merrill, 1974).

at Palau. A surprising number of the Micronesians in authority today are graduates of that school.

The system did produce work for most who wanted it and some who did not, and there is a tendency today among less thoughtful people to remember both the full employment and the firm discipline of the Japanese with some nostalgia. A Japanese foreman knocked down a malingering worker and beat him, but that was the end of it; it is sometimes said that today's discipline, oriented to U.S. civil service procedures, is more baffling and disturbing to some Micronesians. This may be only a theoretical observation, however, since discipline in Micronesia is so rare.

David Ramarui graduated from the Japanese carpentry school at Palau, and in recalling it he touches one of the roots of the problems of today. "The Japanese limited for their own convenience who could go to school; thus we became aliens on our own island. One time we started the Koror Young Men's Association. The Japanese forbade it—we would have to call it the Koror Young Native Men's Association. We like to believe today that democracy must go hand in hand with education and that it allows people to grow without arbitrary limits." The Japanese experience is burned very deeply in Ramarui and in most thoughtful Micronesians. "The schools for Japanese children were excellent. For Palauan children—well, there were eighty-four in my class and the Japanese teacher beat us with a bamboo rod. Japan built the economy, but it did so for Japanese, not for Micronesians. In Koror, no Palauan could own even the smallest store. In Saipan, we heard of no Micronesians in business. Today Joeten [Joe Tenorio, a rather extraordinary Saipanese entrepreneur] is big, big business. Whatever we are today, we are for ourselves—the U.S. gave us that, democracy gave us that."

In 1939 the Japanese military took control of Micronesia, and real preparations for war began. The recent development of heavy bombers made forward land bases important, and four were established on atolls in the Marshalls, the easternmost islands. The Imperial Navy developed an important anchorage in the great lagoon at Truk, and heavy fortifications were built on Saipan. Micronesians were pressed into workgangs, building air fields and fuel dumps. Japan had always held the islands in secrecy, and no word of this construction leaked out. The work was still going on when the fleet struck Pearl Harbor. Guam fell soon afterwards.

The American counterattack came in a two-armed drive aimed ultimately at the Japanese home islands. One came north from the Solomons through New Guinea toward the Philippines. The other struck Tarawa and came through Micronesia to the Marianas and on to the Philippines and Okinawa. The Tarawa invasion fell on November 21, 1943, the first American landing on a well-defended atoll. The boats hung on the reef and casualties were brutal on both sides. Early the next year American troops took Japan's forward bases in the Marshalls, and on February 23, moving west, began bombarding the Marianas—Guam, Tinian, and Saipan.

Japan had 53,000 troops on the three islands, with 30,000 on Saipan alone. They had spent years digging in and were at an emotional peak, expecting to sacrifice themselves—as almost all of them did—before the fighting was over. The American invasion brought 300,000 men to the Marianas on 600 ships—and there is hardly a Micronesian of age today who does not remember the sound of bombers and the crash of shells and the sight of immense fleets standing down the horizon, as far as one could see.

And no one who was there will forget the sight of Saipan at dawn, the mountain spine at its center rising green-black and mysterious. The ships flexed and creaked in the easy water, and the men stood by the guntubs gazing at that implacable mountain, at that dangerous-looking land, and no one said much.

There is still a tank in the lagoon at Saipan, blown out of a boat as it came over the reef. The invaders came across the lagoon and up the beach and the Japanese fell back to well-prepared positions along that terrible mountain spine, and the fighting went on for weeks. Thirty-four hundred Americans died on Saipan and eleven thousand were wounded, and virtually all of the thirty thousand Japanese soldiers perished.

The fear and the fanaticism of the Japanese infected the Saipanese as well, and when the end was certain, Japanese soldiers walked whole Saipanese families to the edge of a cliff, standing one hundred feet over a rock-filled basin where the surf churns and thunders even on the calmest day; so does the island break the Pacific swells. American coxswains brought their craft among the rocks and the piling seas and pleaded over bullhorns for the people to hold fast, but whole families walked backwards off the cliffs and died in the pounding waters below before the small boats could reach them. The last of the Imperial Army moved to the highest cliffs and there the remnants flung themselves off, some marching in formation to the end. Today the waves still howl and slash at the rocks where so many families died, and there is a war memorial erected by the Japanese at the peak of last resistance. It is simple, a bit tattered, weathered by the wet Pacific wind, and now that Saipan at last is open to visitors, tourists from Japan, many of them elderly couples, come to this memorial and stand looking over the sea and hold quiet little services before they turn and go down the steps.

The fighting on Saipan was over on July 9, 1944, and it ended on Guam a month later. The new B-29s, lifting off the long strips on Saipan and Tinian, began firebombing the Japanese home islands. A year later the *Enola Gay* took off from Tinian.

Carrier bombers sank more than sixty ships in that anchorage at Truk, but the invaders bypassed Truk and Yap and struck Palau instead on the way to the Philippines. Marines, backed by the army, landed at Peleliu for some of the bloodiest fighting in the Pacific war, and afterwards angry American troops razed the untouched district center at Koror. To this day Koror has a broken, unfinished look. Thus they cleared the route to the Philippines and to Japan.

Much of the physical infrastructure and certainly the economy of the islands was destroyed in the war, and the United States has done relatively little to replace either. Indeed, one of the most startling things about Micronesia today is that the detritus of war still litters the ground. That tank stands in the lagoon at Saipan, its gun cocked to the sky, its turret askew, and you sit in the hotel and look across the lagoon and wonder if some poor devil died in it. Landing-craft hulks lie half-buried in sand on invasion beaches. Bullet-tattered Japanese fighter aircraft, *Zeroes* caught on the ground, lie beside airstrips on which jets now land. Old cannon serve as decorations, burned tanks lie in fields nearly covered with growth, and old shells still blow up Micronesian children. One of Micronesia's exports long has been the scrap metal of a war now thirty years past. Japanese ships lie on the bottom in Truk Lagoon with masts and superstructures still above the water, so that to look across the sea is to envision it again, the planes flashing over the elephant hump of Dublon Island, the tracer fire and the bomb explosions and the ships twisting in the lagoon like frightened animals. It is depressing: the scars of war should be paved over with affluence, as in the countries that waged it—here, where it was an unsought visitor, its signs remain open and cruel as a burned face.

★
★ ★ **CHAPTER FOUR**
★

THE AMERICAN COLONY

The United States won Micronesia at terrible cost, and that exactly sums up our long-term interest there. That interest is strategic. It was always so and it is today and it will be for the foreseeable future. And it is unmixed. We do not see Micronesia in terms of empire or of economic gain or as a population outlet—we see it solely in terms of the command of the western Pacific that its possession gives any great naval power. With those islands in our hands, we control the breadth of the ocean that washes our western coast and surrounds our fiftieth state. With them out of our hands, our entire world posture changes.

This single, unchanging point is fundamental to everything we have done there and to what we have not done there and to the problems that follow us now like a tracking animal.

Since the Japanese took Micronesia, American planners had pondered the problems of fighting a Pacific war with the islands in the hands of a potential enemy, and the reality was fully as painful as expected. But there was no way to function in the Pacific, no way to return to the Philippines, and certainly no way to challenge Japan itself, without first reducing those terrible bastions. This had been done, the Navy was in control, and the United States had no intention of losing that control.

This attitude was no secret, nor is it today. On February 3, 1947, then Congressman Mike Mansfield of Montana, having returned from a Pacific tour, told the House:

> I would prefer to have the United States assume complete and indisputed control of the Mandates. We need these islands for our future defense, and they should be fortified wherever we deem it necessary. We have no concealed motives because we want these islands for one purpose only and that is national security. . . . No other nation has any kind of claim to the Mandates. No other nation has paid the price we have.

And, presciently, he said:

> Economically they will be a liability, socially they will present problems, and politically we will have to work out a policy of administration.*

As things actually have worked out, the American strategic interest in Micronesia has been served most of all in a negative sense. We maintain big military bases on Guam (from which we bombed North Vietnam), but the actual strategic value of the islands has been denial of their use to any other nation. Guam would be almost worthless—as it was in 1941—if it were surrounded by hostile islands. In practice, then, the United States has made little military use of Micronesia beyond Guam. It maintained a secret CIA

* Congressional Record, Feb. 3, 1947.

base on Saipan in the 1950s, operates a missile-testing range on Kwajalein Atoll in the Marshalls, is considering a new base on Tinian today, and from time to time goes out looking at potential bases, which naturally alarms a people whose total land area is a mere seven hundred square miles.

But the military realities remain quite clear. The military analyst Hanson Baldwin, writing in the *Reader's Digest* in 1971, explained:

> For a number of reasons, the islands of Micronesia are absolutely vital to the long range security of the United States. They extend the potential range of U.S. sea and air power by thousands of miles, yet are not close enough to the continent of Asia to be militarily vulnerable or politically provocative. Except for Guam, they are the only islands in the Western Pacific that fly the American flag, and the only forward-base sites in the Pacific that might substitute in part for Okinawa, the Philippines and Japan. They provide potential early-warning sites for electronics installations to monitor trans-Pacific aircraft and communications. Long-range patrol aircraft, based on these islands, could track Soviet submarines bound for the shipping lanes of the central Pacific. Some of the islands form part of our Pacific missile test range and also offer sites for monitoring Russian missile tests in the Pacific. In a potential enemy's hands, Micronesia would be a strategic nighmare to U.S. defense planners . . .*

A more sophisticated and perhaps more cynical view of U.S. Pacific strategy in the wake of Vietnam appeared in 1972 in the *U.S. Naval Institute Proceedings* by a Marine Corps officer:

> Ours is the hard choice, then, between two hard realities. On the one hand are the fiscal and political

* Hanson W. Baldwin, "Keys to the Pacific," *Reader's Digest*, December 1971.

realities which call for us to abandon our present "forward position" strategy; on the other are the strategic and other political realities which dictate that we must maintain a strong presence in the western Pacific in order to honor treaty commitments and protect national interests. The course we ultimately follow is very likely to be a major change in but not the abandonment of our strategic posture in the western Pacific. . . . A strong probability in the development of a new U.S. role in Asia is for us to fall back from presently occupied "forward positions" to a more consolidated and economical "internal position," from which the same national security goals could be accomplished. The ideal—and perhaps the only—location available for this type of regrouping is the Trust Territory of the Pacific Islands with Guam as a cornerstone.*

But of course there were other factors to be considered in that period after World War II when the United Nations was forming and the world was being reshaped. Old models of colonialism were dying and the question was how the odd bits of territory now coming free were to be handled. The solution was the formation of the United Nations Trusteeship system, designed to govern "a) territories now held under mandate; b) territories which may be detached from enemy states as a result of the Second World War, and c) territories voluntarily placed under the system by states reponsible for their administration." Obviously, that included Micronesia. The Administering Authority of each territory was to "promote the political, economic, social and educational advancement" of the people and to move them as directly as practical toward self-government.

It was clear that the trusteeship system was not to be a means for acquiring territory, which from the beginning

* James H. Webb, Captain, USMC, "Turmoil in Paradise: Micronesia at the Crossroads," *U.S. Naval Institute Proceedings*, July 1972.

put an element of conflict into the U.S. situation. There were eleven trust territories formed; today, the Trust Territory of the Pacific Islands is the only one that has not been resolved. In each case, trusteeship agreement was established between the Administering Authority and the Trusteeship Council, which would monitor the territory and report to the General Assembly.

This amounted to much tighter control than the United States cared for in Micronesia. So it proposed, and the United Nations accepted, a second form—a "strategic" trust territory. Micronesia, as it turned out, was the only strategic trust territory among the eleven. The most important difference is that control rests not in the General Assembly but in the Security Council—where the United States has a veto. In effect, then, the United States can cancel any directive the United Nations may issue on Micronesia. It may exclude whomever it wishes, fortify at will, take land for military purpose through eminent-domain proceedings, and generally act as it likes. So it can afford to take a cavalier view of the United Nations—except when world opinion is involved. "We notify the U.N." one official said, "we don't consult."

In retrospect, the period after World War II was quite naive. It was still easy then to be impressed with our own nobility in international affairs. It was not a day when a president would tell the press that "destabilization" of friendly governments was part of U.S. policy. Yet the difference between what we were and what we said we were— one of the key factors that later seduced us into Vietnam— can be seen in Micronesia from the beginning. We talked about trust agreements and self-government, but we never intended to give up the islands. Congressman Mansfield told his colleagues that while he would prefer outright control, if "it does become necessary to create a trusteeship for these islands, I would favor [the strategic trusteeship, where] and this is important, the United States has a veto over the Security Council should it ever want to assert effective control."*

Much of the confusion in our administration of Micronesia grows from that half-hidden dichotomy of purpose, for it meant that we never faced up clearly to what the future might hold and therefore to what effect our policies might have.

Now, when the United States is under increasing pressure to end the trust agreement and salvage what it can, that old ambivalence becomes dangerous and destructive.

And yet, President Truman certainly was trying to mediate between the strategic realities and the basic desire for things and places to operate under civil and democratic control. The solution in Micronesia represented that compromise. In his memoirs, Truman first discussed Micronesia's strategic significance and then added:

> In earlier meetings with Cabinet members on the question of trusteeships, I found that the State Department held views that differed from those of the War and Navy Departments. I listened carefully to both points of view. In the end I sustained the Army and Navy chiefs on the major issue of the security of the bases. But I also saw the validity of the ideal for which the State Department was contending—that the United Nations should not be barred from the local territories beyond the bases if at any time the United Nations should want to look into the social and economic conditions on these islands. The United States would never emulate the policy of Japan in the areas that were given her under mandate by the League of Nations. We thus assured full protection to our nation against a future Pacific aggressor and, at the same time, laid the foundations for future self-government of the island people.

* Congressional Record, Feb. 3, 1947.

My attitude was always that while it was necessary for us to control certain islands in the Pacific until peace was established, those territories should not be closed to the rest of the world. I believed we should set up civil governments as soon as possible to replace the military governments. Some of the military objected, but while I remained President, I intended to try to get as near to self-government as we could wherever we had the responsibility. . . . I had always been opposed to colonialism.*

Thus civil administration was assured, though it would be several years in coming. In the meantime, however, administration was in the hands of harried naval civil-government teams who moved in behind the troops to take charge of the battered ground and the Micronesians who came out of hiding to greet them.

The Americans tended to see the Micronesians as liberated people, though they had shown few signs of dissatisfaction under thirty years of Japanese rule. But they had survived a hard war in which the people who had dominated them had been smashed and evicted by the newcomers, and it appears that they were amazed and impressed. Certainly they were cooperative, pragmatically accepting the fourth in their long line of rulers.

The Micronesian economy collapsed immediately. The war had destroyed much of the physical plant the Japanese had built, but more importantly, the system itself had been Japanese. When the Japanese were deposed and then repatriated, the Americans found that there was no Micronesian managerial class. Yet dealing with modern systems requires at least a little education, and all at once there was a premium on graduates of that carpentry school, the highest education offered Micronesians. Any Micronesian with a facility for learning English was drawn quickly into the new

* Harry S. Truman, *Memoirs, Vol. I: Year of Decisions* (Garden City, N.Y.: Doubleday, 1955), pp. 274–275.

system. Probably the unflagging Micronesian perception of the value of education began in those tumultuous, frightening days at the end of the war, when for new reasons a new group suddenly began to prosper.

There had been no Micronesian teachers and the schools also collapsed. The Navy added schools to the list of things it had to do and before long it had established a system of universal education to the sixth grade, thus from the beginning doubling the Japanese effort. It set up a system based on three levels of two grades each and expected a school to open in every community. Micronesian teachers were the immediate need, and educators were brought from Hawaii to train them. Hasty classes were set up and likely Micronesians were given six months' tutoring and sent back to their villages and islands to open schools. Probably not much was taught in those early days (nor is all that much taught today), but the idea was implanted. In 1947 the Navy opened the Pacific Islands Teacher Training School at Guam which offered a year of training. The next year it moved the school to Truk and added a second year.

Given the circumstances, merely organizing those schools was a feat, and it is not surprising that what emerged was a reproduction of a weak academic model imported directly from the United States. To this day there has been almost no high-level thought about what Micronesians really need, and certainly there was none at that early point; American schoolmen, operating in awful conditions and under great pressure, just did what they knew how to do. Even then, however, they recognized the problem. A Navy document of the period insists that the system, "although modeled after its American counterpart, is adapted to the conditions and needs peculiar to the islands." It was a nice idea, but it was not true.

The Navy's patchwork system of government gradually hardened into permanence and perpetuated itself so that its approaches are still evident today. When civil control finally came in 1951, it went to the Department of Interior and for years seemed more myth than reality. Interior took the part of a rather bemused—and sorely underfinanced—caretaker without real interests of its own. Military interests, on the other hand, were strong and unchanging. The first contest came over the territorial headquarters, which the Navy had maintained at Honolulu. Interior thought that Saipan was the logical site. It was centrally located and there were ample facilities which the Navy had abandoned—airstrips, docks, buildings, warehousing, utilities. But the Navy resisted, the issue was delayed, the facilities began to disintegrate, and in the end Trust Territory headquarters remained in Honolulu, some two thousand miles from the nearest Trust Territory island. In a little more than a year the Navy had regained control of the Marianas, and it kept Interior out for another decade. Presumably this was related to the Naval Technical Training Unit, which the Central Intelligence Agency established on Saipan to train foreign nationals for espionage against their own governments. One can still walk down the overgrown airstrip on which C-47s touched down in the dark with loads of young Chinese from Taiwan; they were blindfolded, so one common story goes, so that when they were captured later and tortured, they could not reveal where they had been trained. Little is known of this operation even today, but it is believed that hundreds of young men were parachuted into China, where they were soon captured, and other countries may have been targeted as well. But one can see the extent of the operation in the base iself, which, with a certain irony, ultimately became headquarters for the Trust Territory government after the whole territory was opened radically in 1962. It is cunningly set atop the highest mountain on the island so that it is visible only from the air; and it invariably surprises visitors. Its concrete buildings are big and elaborate, if dark with mildew, and its tract-like homes are set out on wide streets and ample lawns; it might be an old military base in California, now seedy and half-deserted.

Despite the ostensible civil control of all but the

Marianas, the whole of Micronesia remained under military security through the 1950s. No doubt this secrecy was in part to protect the atomic tests conducted in the Marshalls and the missile station developed at Kwajalein, but since the Marshalls are removed from the bulk of Micronesia, the real cause probably was no more than the military penchant for secrecy and control. No one could enter the Trust Territory without permission. Even Department of Interior officials needed a specific Navy clearance to land at Guam, which was the starting place to visit the territory they were administering. When Trust Territory headquarters moved to Guam in 1954, still not in the territory itself, the restrictions continued. Visiting United Nations teams were admitted, but other foreign nationals were barred automatically. So rare were exceptions that the territory's 1958 annual report noted almost proudly: "A Trukese-Japanese, born at Truk and sent to Japan at an early age, was granted permission to visit his family at Truk and his temporary permit was extended for a year in accordance with clearance granted by the Navy. This was the culmination of several years of effort by the man and his relatives for permission to visit his mother and other members of his family in the Trust Territory."

This long period of isolation continued the Japanese policy of barring foreigners and bears directly on the unreality that now afflicts the territory. For years the people there were allowed only American models for dealing with the modern technological world, and though the situation has opened somewhat, American models still predominate. And as one might expect, they really are not appropriate to the underdeveloped tropical specks of Micronesia.

Companion to the military isolation was the civil stagnation. For the first ten years of its duty, the territorial government under Interior did as little as possible. Its resources were slight but the point is that it did not seek to do more, and toward the end of the period it was reducing its scale.

The territory was headed by a high commissioner who

was appointed by the President but reported to the secretary of interior. Gradually a territorial bureaucracy developed and the high commissioner became increasingly independent. A decade later, when Interior wanted to assert
control, it found it had a fight on its hands; and even today
the high commissioner seems to treat with Washington only
in formal terms.

Separated from Washington (which usually ignored it),
limited by modest budgets, the territorial government simply tried to maintain what the Navy had established. It was
not a period for new ideas, nor is there sign that any were
present. It was problem enough just getting around the
huge territory. The Navy had released four old PBY am-
phibious aircraft and seven small ships. The planes flew a
halting schedule among the six district centers and the
ships limped from island to island. Yet every year the territory spent nearly a quarter of its entire budget on transportation alone.

Many of the territory's administrators had served first
with the Navy, and naturally they continued what had gone
before. Out in the districts, they tended to be on their own
and thus to follow their own inclinations. There rarely were
more than three hundred American employees, and the figure shrank as the decade wore on. Administrators from
headquarters rarely visited the districts. Travel was too difficult and too expensive, which remains true, to some extent, today. The Americans in the districts lived in compounds, and much of their efforts at improvement were
aimed at these compounds. Micronesians have developed a
certain cynicism, and it was not lost on them that most
roads and water lines reached no farther than the American
compounds and that most power plants produced little
excess voltage. As so often happens in colonial situations,
the colonizers came to resent the native peoples. They were
slow, they didn't speak English, they thought differently.
William Vitarelli remembers an administrator at Palau

shouting, "The trouble with this goddamned place is that there are too many Palauans here!"

As Japanese money had gone to Japanese, so Americans spent on Americans. Headquarters spent about half the total budget. The other half, divided among six districts, certainly was spent in the main on construction, comforts, and salaries for Americans. Only a little trickled down to the people, in the form of subsistence salaries and occasional public-works projects.

The bulk of the territory's funding comes from the U.S. Congress, which at that point had a $7.5 million limit on the annual appropriation. The territory's requests never approached that figure. The actual budget, which included about $1.5 million in local revenues (mostly from transportation and other user fees), hovered a little above $6 million.

The budget was static through the 1950s despite inflation and a growing population. A census in 1952 showed 57,037 Micronesians, less than half of today's population. By 1958 the figure had risen more than 17 percent to 67,199. Yet the budget, having reached a high of $6.9 million in 1956, dropped steadily thereafter and in 1960 stood at $5.9 million.

There was almost no serious construction. The infrastructure the Japanese had created was not restored. Buildings and equipment became steadily more dilapidated as maintenance funds shrank. There were few visitors, and so there was little need for hotels. Patsy Mink, the congresswoman from Honolulu, recalls being given a hotel room at Majuro that had no windows. A merchant captain who had been there during the war went back a decade later and observed, "It was like going back into the war. It was amazing. The only hotels were old barracks, the only trading company was the one the Navy had established. Nothing had changed." The somnolent quality increased.

When the economy collapsed after the war, government-owned commercial firms took over the day-to-day com-

merce upon which a society depends. By 1955, trading com-
panies had been organized in each district. Altogether they
did some $2 million a year in local trade; but considering
the vicissitudes of trade in Micronesia, success meant
breaking even.

The Navy, consistent to its own interests (which were
anything but commercial), was quite frank about Micronesia's limited financial potential. A 1948 document observed:

> The natural resources of the islands are meager,
> though they will sustain the local island peoples rea-
> sonably well. There are limited opportunities for fu-
> ture expansion and development. Furthermore [the]
> islands cannot be expected to be self-supporting. . . .
> [they] are a liability and an inevitable charge on the
> public purse.*

There was no industry, no manufacturing, and almost no
commercial agriculture. The cane plantations of the Japanese were long destroyed, and they had been commercially
viable only for a nation that was desperate for sugar. Micronesian sugar could not possibly compete on world markets. The only cash crop remaining was copra, and, as one
report noted sadly, "An economy based on copra is notably
unstable, for the world price fluctuates violently."†

About twelve thousand tons of Micronesian copra were
sold in 1952, marketed for a small percentage by a San Francisco firm. In 1955 the government organized a stabilization
fund to set aside income when the price was high in order
to maintain payments of about $100 a ton to producers
when the world price was low. That figure proved popular—it meant that an islander could count on five dollars
for a hundred-pound bag. It was neat, certain, and risk-
free, and Micronesians like that.

* Trust Territory of the Pacific Islands, Honolulu, *Handbook*, 1948.
† Trust Territory of the Pacific Islands, Honolulu, *Annual Report*, 1952.

The administration began trying to improve the copra crop. It invited a coconut expert from the South Pacific Commission to tour the islands and to make recommendations. One year a Director of Coconut Operations was appointed to help the people improve their crop. Perhaps the title came uncomfortably close to summing up the whole territorial operation; in later reports, the Director no longer appeared. A seedling nursery was established, the best planting depths and tree spacing were determined, fertilizers were imported, and pamphlets full of coconut advice were distributed. But year after year the sale crop ranged from twelve to thirteen thousand tons, less when there were serious typhoons.

The territory continued to speculate and to hope. Perhaps coffee would grow on the high islands. Or pepper. Or cacao—now, *there* was a possibility. An ambitious cacao project was started, with a laboratory and a seedling nursery that ultimately produced millions of trees. They were planted and a few even bore, but year by year there was some new problem to overcome, and at last the cacao project faded from view. Most Micronesians of the time lived in part by subsistence fishing, and toward the end of the 1950s there began the first of the fisheries projects which would bring officials so much frustration and Micronesians so little fish.

It was, in short, poor—just as it always had been, just as it is today.

And Americans understood that well enough at the time. Looking back from today's viewpoint, the American attitude was a curious blend of an appealing grasp of reality (appealing particularly because it is so absent today) and colonial paternalism as blind as most colonial views. It recognized clearly that Micronesians could not support an American lifestyle on their own resources, and it forecast accurately what would happen if the lifestyle simply was furnished them. There is a note of real prophecy today in the admonitions then common on the relationship between real work and real return. "We are concentrating priority on the Micronesian subsistence economy," an economic advisor told Robert Trumbull in 1958. "Before introducing new elements in the economy, we must upgrade what they already have here. We want the Micronesian to eat better of his local produce rather than become dependent on food that is shipped in."*

In *A Reporter in Micronesia*, E. J. Kahn quoted an economist writing in 1952 about equalizing salaries, though his point applies much more broadly. The man noted that "care should be exercised, as it has been so far, not to advance wages beyond all reasonable hope that the productivity of the economy will be enough to sustain such wages. This is no idle caveat. Wage reasoning shaped by the cry of discrimination or by comparison with American wages would be ruinous to the Trust Territory economy in its present stage of productivity."† The statement would stand as well today, of course, just by changing the tense from future to past.

But no one seemed to understand that change was inevitable as the Micronesians moved into the modern world. The only way to deal with change is to help it come in realistic ways. Instead, High Commissioner Delmas H. Nucker could tell Trumbull rather smugly in 1958, "There are no signs of famine, social unrest or distress, poverty or niggardly living in Micronesia. So long as the people are learning and living a reasonably happy and healthful life, to give them the blessings of advanced American civilization would be to cause more problems. Unrest would grow faster than we could handle it."‡ And things were quieter then. The radical population shift to the district centers that is becoming critical today had not yet begun. And considering the shocking imbalance today of imports that run ten

* Trumbull, p. 209.
† E. J. Kahn, Jr., *A Reporter in Micronesia* (New York: Norton, 1966), p. 119.
‡ Trumbull, p. 211.

times exports and more, the imbalance of that period was modest. In 1958, for example, imports were $3.4 million and exports were $2.2 million.

It was simple colonial arrogance: the superior people knew best, the inferior people were to stay on their islands for—for how long? That was the question that no one would address, though the impulses that today are at such a dangerous point in Micronesia were already moving then.

The same attitude controlled the education system that the Navy had started on urban American lines after the war and that the civil administration inherited without thought of change. Restraint was the key word. education awakens minds in and out of classrooms, and the fear was that too much would be done, that expectations would be inflated beyond reason, and that the result would turn out to be exactly what, in fact, it has been. This appraisal of the island's potential was accurate enough, but it is strange that even in education, where surely ideas should be welcome, everyone seemed to assume that no other forces were at work and that the pastoral island life would go on forever.

Robert Gibson, education director during the 1950s, fought so hard for restraint that when the decision was made in the 1960s to reverse the policy, the next step was to push him into retirement. He is a spare, slender man, now in his seventies and living in Honolulu, a professional educator who came into colonial service, so to speak, when he headed an education program for the Americans of Japanese extraction who were interned in California; if he feels any retrospective regrets today, he does not include them in a discussion of his background. After the war he went to Korea as an advisor to the government on education, and in 1951 he came to Micronesia to take over the Navy-developed education system. And, after the fashion of the period, he carried on.

In a perceptive essay circulated in typescript, Francis Hezel quotes Macaulay on the purpose of education in India, "to produce men who are Indian in color and blood,

but English in tastes, in opinions, in morals and in intellect
. . ." No doubt the American view is less openly colonial,
but the effect is similar. Schools inevitably reinforce culture:
schools in America Americanize students. This was more
obvious when public schools were assimilating immigrant
children into American life, but it is still in school that
youngsters get the sense of their culture and their national
heritage, that their attitudes and expectations and proprie-
ties are perfected. As change shakes the American society
and therefore its schools, that remains true even if the perceptions the child receives alarm his parents. So, Hezel observes, it is hardly surprising that American schools in Micronesia, with their outward focus on individual
achievement, tended to Americanize students.

Everyone understood this, but the common assumption
was that Micronesia's future was with the United States
anyway, so what did it matter? Meller, certainly the ranking
political scientist in the Pacific, thinks that teaching American values was expected to bind people closer. But this is
dangerous—and in one sense, unconscionable—for as Micronesian youngsters become more American they certainly
are less Micronesian. Yet the idea of an American future
was never more than a vague policy hope formulated in situation rooms in Washington, where people are abstractions
and the power games of great war-machines are reality.

There were about 7,000 students in the 144 public elementary schools the new territorial administration took
from the Navy. At least half of these had but one teacher,
often in an open-walled thatched shed, and reached only to
the third grade. A few elementary students went on to intermediate schools, grades seven to nine (theoretically),
which had a total enrollment in all districts of about six
hundred. Micronesian students tended to be older than the
grades suggest; intermediate students ranged from eighteen
to twenty-five.

Parochial schools, mostly Catholic, had another two thousand students. These schools are still important and still re-

ceive government assistance, but the most interesting thing about them is that with a single important exception, they are a bit better but otherwise are not different than the public schools. Answers do not come easily in Micronesia.

There were 266 public school teachers that first year. Most were youngsters who had been trained hastily on Guam. Communities were uninterested in formal education then and considered anyone under forty as hardly worth hearing, so the schools had slow going. But gradually, as American educators went from community to community describing the blessings of education, local pride began to grow around the school. This was fortunate, since each community was expected to build and maintain the school and support the teacher.

There were never more than thirty Americans on the education staff, in the districts and at headquarters, which was located at Truk. The budget permitted little travel. It was hard to know whether a teacher was even holding school, let alone how many grades were open. The standards of the period really were goals; reports noted carefully that the system has six grades "when feasible" in the particular community.

The education budget ranged from five to nine percent of the territory total, from less than $300,000 to just over $500,000. So strong was the policy of leaving responsibility for grade schools to the community that the department budgeted only $9,164 for elementary education in the first year, of a total budget of $392,000. Gradually support for school construction went up, and eventually there was some salary support.

The shortage of trained teachers was overwhelming. The few American teachers were too precious to waste on children: they trained other teachers, sometimes roving far among the outer islands to do so. One of these trainers was a colorful woman named Cicely Pickerill, then in her sixties, who toured the islands of Truk in a small boat, often carrying a canvas bathtub as her only concession to her own national outlook. Mrs. Pickerill kept a diary which gives a dismaying sense of the schools she encountered, and she let Robert Trumball quote from it.

"Some villages had a school day of about forty minutes," she wrote after visiting one island. "The teachers had to walk long distances, carrying all their materials each time. Besides, the people were not interested in the school. The teachers were too young and had no prestige. They got discouraged."

"Teachers are trying to teach things beyond themselves," she observed at another point. "Teachers are unable to implement what they have learned. They have very little formal education and don't know what or how to teach."

But it was the schools themselves that most bothered her. "Some schools were in old, completely bombed-out Japanese structures. The people began to repair these only last year. Some were in thatched buildings completely open to the weather, with the blackboards leaning against poles. Rain would send the children scurrying to the farthest corners for shelter. I have seen storms in which the wind blew the pencils and papers out of the children's hands and scattered all working materials on the sand. When the children lost their pencils there were no more to be had. Some schools had no yardsticks or rulers. The pupils sat on the sand or dirt or a rough concrete floor. Imagine trying to write on a single sheet of paper on such a floor!"*

Perhaps the most dismaying point in Mrs. Pickerill's obviously warm-hearted concern is not what bothered her but rather the image of the Americanized education perservering no matter how remote and difficult the conditions. Indeed, the schools of the period, with their standard curriculum of reading, figuring, social studies, and science, seem to have made but a single concession to the fact that the students were Micronesians. Though other Americans often demanded Why don't you teach these people proper En-

* Trumbull, p. 119 ff.

glish? Gibson insisted that training must start in the child's native language. He believed that severing a child from his language undermines his grasp of his own culture. For the first four grades, teaching was entirely in the vernacular, with English introduced as a course in grades five and six. In the end Gibson lost this battle too—so completely that today, when the concept is returning clothed in fresh theories about the assassination of culture through deprivation of language, it is regarded as an exciting new departure.

But given the budget of the period and the quality of the teachers, it is hard to see what else he could have done. And it is doubtful that anything like English was available even in fifth and sixth grades. "That was my policy," Gibson says today, adding carefully, "Of course, it was hard to be sure how much it was implemented in the outer islands because it was so hard to get out there to see."

William Vitarelli, who went to Palau in 1949 to head education there and in Yap for the Navy, learned early how difficult was the reality of introducing English. In 1950, he visited his first outer-island school, at Mog Mog in Ulithi Atoll. Vitarelli is an articulate, forthright, rather iconoclastic man, and to this day he remembers his shock:

"We landed at Mog Mog and I walked into a thatched classroom. It had nine kids all sitting on a bench, each with a book. The teacher handed me one of the books, and my God, it was the same thing they were using in Bucks County, Pennsylvania. The kids stood up and they all sang in unison, 'Good morning,' and I said, 'Good morning.' It was a primer and the title was Dick and Jane. Really. My own kid, Sandy, had used the same book at Horace Mann Lincoln School in New York. The teacher had them line up and they started to read in unison, 'Run, Dick, run!' I was so impressed—negatively—that this copy was identical, that this was the same thing educators were doing in the states. But there, you know, it had some relevancy for the children. See the father with a briefcase, the suburban street, the kid on a tricycle—what relevance did it have here? And when they were all done they stood there smiling and looking pleased with themselves, and what could I say? So I spoke to the teacher. 'Congratulations,' I said, and I was going to add something when his face went blank. 'Huh?' he said, and it dawned on me that he didn't understand any English. He had been to Guam for three months' training and he had learned to read the lines in the primer and he had taught the sounds to the children by memory, and neither he nor the kids had any idea what they meant. That was rote learning."

There really was not much way for a Micronesian teacher to teach in English. Teaching the subjects of a radically different culture was difficult enough in itself without doing so in a language one did not understand. Even those who could read some English still explained in their own language, and this tends to be true today.

Starting in the vernacular put a premium on almost nonexistent materials. Gradually the territory acquired small presses in various districts which turned out pamphlet-like readers in the local languages. One early Chamorran reader, for example, was called *Atan! Atan!—Look! Look!*—and really was a standard American Dick-and-Jane translated literally—with little place indeed in which the island children could see themselves. The lack of materials in the vernacular thrust still more of the teaching burden onto those untrained teachers, since they had to operate almost without guidance.

The decade of the 1950s was a quiescent period, with the bureaucratic tone that made the whole territory so western marking the schools as well. The education department was dedicated enough, but it usually was easier to do things by the book. Vitarelli, who holds a doctorate from Columbia and to this day retains the vitality and imagination that led him to a long career as gadfly, stinging the Trust Territory administration again and again, was one of the few exceptions.

"Bob Gibson was conceptually liberal," Vitarelli said, "but I think it scared him to see things happening. We didn't get into English until the fifth grade in those days so we had no syllabus for the first four grades, a real shortage of material in the Palauan language. So in the school at Palau, to try to make education specific and related, we started a garden and we sold produce in the market. The kids loved it and they worked hard and we tied it right into their studies, arithmetic, writing, everything. In those days the community paid the teachers, and there was lots of local interest in the school. So the people flocked to the market, and it was a real market, real selling, done by the kids, and that's how we got money for books. And Bob came down, and of course he was impressed by the enthusiasm, but then he took me aside and said, 'Don't you know its against the rules for public schools to sell things?' So we had to drop the market. Instead he wanted me to concentrate on getting specifics on the number of kids in classes. We had been sending estimates, you see, there being no exact anything in Micronesia, and he wanted exactness.

"And in about 1953 a man came down to Palau from Interior to look us over. And he was impressed with the schools we had built and the community enthusiasm and the way the kids were learning. But we sat down that weekend and he said, 'You're doing a good job here—but now you have to get down to real school.' Schools geared to the community need just made him uneasy—'How will these kids compete?' he kept asking. Everything he thought seemed geared to the States. My God, he talked as though Palau was a colony or even already a state. We must train people to be good Americans, that sort of thing. And gradually, the things we were doing that seemed to me to relate the kids to the community and the environment just faded away."

There really was only one bright spot in education, not because it was excellent, which it was not, but because it made sense. The Pacific Islands Central School, known always as PICS, was small, poorly equipped, shabbily quartered and understaffed—and it appears to have worked. It was the territory's only public institution of higher learning, though for most of its life it stopped short of being a full high school. It opened as the Pacific Islands Teacher Training School at Guam, changed its name (though teacher training remained its basic mission), moved to Truk for most of its life, and finally went to Ponape not long before it was allowed to die. At that point it had added a third year to its basic two-year course.

It usually had 120 students drawn 60 per year from all the districts. Theoretically they were drawn on merit, a point Gibson insists on today, but there often was a bit more to the choice. There usually is in Micronesia. Petrus Tun, who represents Yap in the senate of the Congress of Micronesia and chairs its education committee, told me he was quite surprised when he was chosen for PICS by his teacher, who happens now to be the other senator from Yap. Later I learned that Tun's family is such as to make his selection quite obvious. Most of the students were beyond high school age, ranging up to thirty-five, and at one point a couple of outer-island chiefs were students. They were an elite group, by blood or by intellect and quite often by both.

The school was small and simple. It stood on a bluff overlooking the Truk lagoon; in the distance another island was rimed in surf. Two over-sized Quonset huts, set side to end in an L-shape beside a playing field, were the heart of the school. One was an auditorium and the other was cut into several classrooms. Students lived in a cluster of small Quonsets nearby.

The school never had more than seven teachers and often was down to four. Most teachers were dependent wives of Americans stationed at Truk, which was cheaper but meant that often they were not well trained. But they were American and spoke English as their native language, which may have been their most important qualifications.

Class opened daily at 7:30 A.M. with a ninety-minute core

class, sort of a home-room grouping about which the rest of the school was organized. This class stressed social sciences, health, economics, and politics and was always popular, since living on a small island is a political act and Micronesians tend to be natural politicians. Class continued until noon with math, English, a little science, and what Lola Smith, who taught there at the time, called "experimental—experimental because we were trying to figure out what would be best for a Micronesian education." Then there were vocational electives with special emphasis on agriculture, but including sewing, bookkeeping, typing, and occasionally mechanics. Most of the books were American readers, grades four to six, and tattered nearly beyond recognition. Naturally they had little bearing on Micronesia, but they were the sort of things from which the students ultimately would be teaching. Mrs. Smith remembers that they started a typing class with a single typewriter and slowly built up to several, keeping the machines in a light locker against the tropic damp and battling administrators who wondered why they should waste good typewriters on a school. "But that was typical—the whole plant was rundown, supplies were short, books were a disgrace. The food was deplorable—every commissary day you heard people pressing the tops of cans to see if they were swollen—ping-ping, ping-ping."

And yet, shabby as it was, PICS worked. It was a real success, one of the few successes the territory has known, and wherever you go in Micronesia, people speak of it with nostalgia and affection. I never met a PICS graduate who didn't recall it with pleasure, and as for the American teachers—"It was a joy to teach there," Mrs. Smith said, sitting in her kitchen in Washington, D. C., two decades later. "I didn't go into education when we came home because I was sure I couldn't find a place so marvelous to teach. The kids were eager and happy. They were an elite, they certainly were, and they were smart and they helped the learning process along. Our headaches were never with students—problems were always with budgets or personnel or scheduling. I think it was so marvelous because we were accomplishing what we were trying to do and we knew it and the students knew it. The faculty was unified and creative and we were filled with idealism. Whatever may have happened since out there, even if we were naive in our assumptions, even if it couldn't have lasted, that was a successful school. Real learning was going on."

PICS fell short even of the high school level, but it was by far the best public education in Micronesia, and it was the doorway for the best students to go on to college. Only a few managed college in that early period, and they had to prepare themselves further. One of the brightest PICS graduates, and one of Micronesia's most able leaders today, is Kaleb Udui of Palau, who went from PICS to the Mid-Pacific Institute in Honolulu and from there to George Washington University in Washington, D. C., for undergraduate work and for a law degree. Today he is Counsel to the Congress of Micronesia, and he remains in affectionate contact with Cicely Pickerill, who was principal of PICS at the time and who, with others, recognized his capacities and saw that his education continued.

And PICS had that kind of impact at a number of levels. Since the students came from different districts, they faced for the first time a real imperative to learn English. Udui, whose teachers remember his English as superior, himself remembers it this way: "When I went to PICS I thought I would never master English. I would think in Palauan and then try to translate it into English, to construct sentences bit by bit. It was slow, but you had no choice." Students from all districts were scattered through the classes. The teachers were Americans—the first real contact with Americans that most students had—and they had to teach in English since they could hardly master the several languages. Even more important, students had to speak English to each other, since each district's language is different. Udui still remembers what a relief it was to cluster with a group of

Palauans in the evening and lapse into the familiar language.

This was the first time that most students had encountered Micronesians from other districts, and it certainly was at PICS that the idea of Micronesia as an entity began to grow among an educated elite. Micronesia had never been an entity to its own people—the term Micronesia itself was foreign, as was the concept. Under the Japanese, Micronesians were not encouraged to think at all—and certainly not about themselves in nationalistic terms. Under the Americans, the islands first were united politically, and it was at PICS that the leaders of the future began to sense the real meaning of that unity. Almost all of Micronesia's leaders today are graduates of that battered old school.

Recognizing their leadership potential, the school consciously set out to introduce its students to democratic political modes. In the traditional culture, decisions were made by consensus channeled through various forms of clan royalty, and in the pre-American colonial days, decisions were not left to Micronesians. Under the Americans, therefore, new forms had to evolve, and student government became a basic part of PICS training. It began in those core classes, which were the representative units of the government. They generally contained students from every district, so the students could not lapse into district—that is, national—chauvinism and were forced to follow democratic forms. The government that resulted had no more real power than its counterparts elsewhere, but the concepts it developed can be seen today in the democratically elected district legislatures and in the Congress of Micronesia.

As you look back across the long, quiescent period of the 1950s in Micronesia, PICS seems the only thing that makes much sense. It was not that it fit the culture—indeed, it was at pains to educate to the western world that lay out beyond Micronesia's rolling horizons—but that it was real. If Micronesia was to deal with the future, it needed a cadre who understood the nature of the future. Inevitably that meant an elite, but it also opened the possibility for those it touched to deal in reality. The root problem with education in Micronesia was that it bore no real relation to the lives and to the future of the people receiving it. And unreality creates its own disaster.

★ ★ ★ CHAPTER FIVE

THE NEW FRONTIER
TO ACTION

In 1960 the Trust Territory lay dormant under the blazing sun, its American caretakers moving slowly through days of routine, without plan or apparent purpose. Population was at almost seventy thousand and the budget was steady. High Commissioner Delmas Nucker assured a congressional subcommittee that there would be "no major changes as proposed in our activities in 1961 over 1960." The end of the Eisenhower period focused on holding down budgets. A few more elementary schools were built, but the chief educational concern that year was the schools Nucker wanted to establish for the handful of American dependent children. His budgets left little for maintenance, and throughout the territory the buildings and equipment and jeeps inherited from the Navy a decade before were disintegrating. Wags called it the Rust Territory. Airplanes still landed in lagoons for lack of landing strips. Headquarters remained at Guam, and the Navy still held all of Micronesia in tight security and still controlled Saipan, where the big CIA base was being phased out. Of course everyone in the territory accepted the mandate of the United Nations to improve health and education and to move the people toward economic and political self-sufficiency. The question was how fast should it go, and the answer was slowly.

Into this somnolent life came the new Kennedy Administration, blazing with impatience, demanding change, motion, action. It is a little hard to remember now the enthusiasm we brought to that period—we had not yet been treated to that terrible burlesque of ourselves, "I am the greatest!" All we had to do was get the country moving again. Impatience was the new order. Change now and pay later—there was nothing that young men of goodwill and vigor, the new generation tempered in war and trained in prosperity, couldn't do with their energy and management precision and fourteen-hour days. It wasn't even hard. If you had the right instincts you knew what to do and now, like the daydreams of childhood realized, the way was open. The change that followed these attitudes crashed through Micronesia like cannon fire and was approximately as discriminate in whom it touched.

Micronesia was just the place to demonstrate the New Frontier manner. It was so tiny in proportion to its patron that relatively few dollars could produce startling results. It was dependent. It was our legal and moral responsibility. It was a potential American showplace—and much easier to control than recalcitrant places like Vietnam. From Washington's perspective it was natural to go ahead; indeed, it was inevitable.

This thrust focused in the Department of Interior, though it had important elements at State, at Defense, and at the White House. Stewart Udall was secretary and a professional new-frontiersman. Under him was a man who came to regard Micronesia as a minor mission, John A. Carver, Jr., assistant secretary for public land management. He commanded a total of six bureaus, most of them with multimillion dollar budgets and employee rolls to match, but it was the Office of Territories that stole his heart. Carver, now a law professor at the University of Denver, once administrative assistant to Frank Church of Idaho, long had been interested in territories, especially Alaska and Hawaii, which had recently been admitted to statehood. Carver brought in Robert Mangan, then a Department of Defense theorist, as his deputy; now he regards Mangan as "the intellectual leader" of the Micronesia policies. Soon command of the Office of Territories whould be assumed by Ruth Van Cleve, a strong, intelligent lawyer who handled territorial affairs in Interior's solicitor's office.

Territories included Guam, Samoa, the Virgin Islands, Puerto Rico. The Trust Territory was an appendage. Territories are fun, Carver once said. They amount to real control instead of jurisdiction over warring bureaus. "You can get into real problems, people problems, like in little towns." The secretary—or his assistant—ultimately is chief executive, chief legislator, chief justice. "The scope is narrow, but within it he is as strong as anything in the system. We usually divide power, but not in territories."

"Carver was the force behind it," Van Cleve said. "He found those little units of government fascinating."

"We all found them fascinating," Mangan said. "You could deal with them, you could know what was going on. We spent a disproportionate amount of time on territories— and considering that the Trust Territory was the least, we certainly spent a disproportionate amount on it."

Interior's structural approach to territories had grown out of the fact that most of them became states. Since their people were moving toward self-government within the American system, they should have as much local control as possible. This democratic thrust was very strong in the new administration. Washington stands ready to help, Carver told an audience in Guam, in a speech he now feels stands for his policy, "but the power to decide remains with you, through [your] political institutions. . . ." Reeling off the

names of territorial capitals, he explicitly linked the Trust
Territory to his view of territories, and continued, "We
learn as much from our mistakes as from correct decisions
. . . More fundamentally, the right to decide includes the
right to be wrong! Actions to limit the latter, however noble
in their conception, work an erosion of the basic philoso-
phy. Progress toward total competence in the art of government must not be impeded by over-solicitous guardianship
which isolates the political body from the experience of
being mistaken."

Reflecting today, he added, "I had a strong feeling that
that kind of big brotherism was just inconsistent with the
Kennedy Administration." This focus on the American territorial ideal, however, made real problems for the Trust
Territory. It was not the same as an American territory. Its
people were not Americans, nor were they necessarily des-
tined to become Americans. The policy assumes development in an open society, but Micronesia was still closed. It
remained coerced by the military, a carefully maintained
backwater where experience with the modern world was
limited and impressions were filtered through a metropolitan American viewpoint. Indeed, considering the change
then before Micronesia, the American attitude was an easy
out. America would provide the means to produce radical
change—but at the same time it would shift responsibility
for the terms of the change to people who were poorly
equipped to deal with it. It is not up to us, Americans were
saying rather piously, to tell them how to run their lives.
Americans are still saying that today, as the results of the
last decade become ever more evident.

Meanwhile the man who would carry out the new ideas
was being appointed quite independently of Carver. M. W.
Goding became High Commissioner of the Trust Territory
in March 1961, about the time that Carver was appointed
and long before plans for Micronesia began to form. His
views on Micronesia, to the extent that he had any, were
not at issue. The post carried a GS-18 rank, a height that

civil servants rarely reach without political support. Will Goding was from Alaska and had had a long association with Senator E. L. Bartlett of Alaska. His sister was Bartlett's secretary. And he was well enough qualified. He had joined the territorial government in Alaska in 1944 and Interior itself in 1946 and had moved creditably through the bureaucracy. He was in line, Bartlett was an early John F. Kennedy supporter, and he got the job.

But in fact, he was not a new frontiersman in style or outlook or approach. He was a bureaucrat—a stolid, rather cautious man of forty-nine who was not imaginative or creative or very forceful. "He wasn't flashy," a friend said, "and some flash was desirable in the Kennedy administration." He was always a little out of step with the swift movers in Washington, and because he also was tough and stubborn, Assistant Secretary Carver and others began to find him frustrating. But Goding was appointed by the President, and though he reported to the secretary, he knew how to exploit his considerable independence. Interior asked him much more often than it told him.

Goding went out immediately to visit his new charge. When he was ready to depart Honolulu on a Pan American flight for Guam, he was handed a clearance from the Chief of Naval Operations. He was standing with Bill Daniel, the newly appointed governor of Guam and brother of Texas Governor Price Daniel. Goding remembers that Daniel refused his clearance. "I don't need any clearance; I'm the governor of the place," he said. When the naval officer insisted, Daniel got angry. "Look," he said, "I'm appointed by the President and confirmed by the Senate. I don't need CNO permission to go to my own post—I won't accept it." The incident is important because the Navy's secrecy policy was increasingly untenable—and that would force rethinking of everything.

At about the same time, Carver and his deputy, Robert Mangan, toured all the territories, including Micronesia. Naturally they were startled by Micronesia; visitors today are still startled by the strange combination of battered buildings and a disoriented society under a standard American overpresence.

"I remember going into a native school at Truk," Mangan said. "It had a high roof and a weatherbeaten look and the kids sat on a dirt floor. The teacher had been to PICS and the kids were learning everything by rote because there were no books, just a few pamphlets in Trukese."

They went on to PICS and, fresh from Washington, missed whatever dedication was there. "You got the feel immediately, the atmosphere. There was little sense of accomplishment. Yet here was the leadership formation place for the whole territory. The level of English was awful but the only place to go from here was Guam or Hawaii and there the language problem would be compounded. Communication even among kids was a major problem—the district groups all separated outside the classroom. I just couldn't see this as a democratizing, nation-building center."

Goding reacted similarly. Upon seeing his first school, he told a reporter later, "I felt like weeping."

The unsettling experience crystallized decision in Carver and Mangan. This place needed rebuilding, that was all there was to it, and what better place to start than on those pitiful schools? Nor did Goding disagree. "We had lots of talks about it," Mangan said, "and Goding was more willing on this than on lots of things that came later. Will just wasn't a boat-rocker, that's all. He was really interested in improving transportation among the islands—that's what seemed to bother him most."

While thus they speculated, the United Nations dropped a small bomb in their midst. In the spring of 1961 a United Nations visiting mission toured Micronesia, as missions had regularly since the trust was established. Until now, however, the mission reports had been innocuous. But the United Nations was changing too. In 1960 sixteen new states entered the United Nations and the balance of power

shifted to the third world. Late that year the General Assembly passed the "Declaration on the Granting of Independence to Colonial Countries and Peoples" which has
controlled the issue of colonialism ever since. Washington,
which at that time still appeared to take the United Nations
seriously, was, as Max Frankel put it in *The New York Times*,
"making new efforts to convey an enlightened position on
'colonialism' issues." So when the 1961 visiting mission
was organized under Carlos Salamanca of Bolivia, it took its
duties more seriously then earlier missions seem to have
done and delivered a thorough report. It was not highly
critical, but any criticism struck U.S. authorities as a bomb-
shell. It called for "greater and speedier effort" to prepare
Micronesia for self-determination and attacked the United
States for its failure to develop the territory economically.
Rather ironically, one of the few favorable points it found
was the universality of elementary education. This compli-
mentary rose amidst the thorns probably had a conditioning effect in the decision to hurtle forward in education.

But what most seems to have stung—and alarmed—
American policymakers was the mission's statement that it
had found "considerable dissatisfaction and discontent"
among the islanders. Discussing the subject years later on
the floor of the Senate, it was this that Mike Mansfield remembered, the single point of "considerable dissatisfaction
and discontent." Nor was it a matter of empty pride, for it
went to the heart of the American position. The United
States intended to stay in Micronesia, and it needed the
people of Micronesia on its side to do so, since legally it
could acquire the islands only if Micronesians voted in a
plebiscite to join the United States. Discontented islanders
could smash all its plans. In the highest councils of the
American government there began a serious reexamination
of American goals in Micronesia and how best to realize
them. Included in this study was the strict secrecy which
the military still imposed on the territory, a point that may
not have been unrelated to Bill Daniel's complaints about

the naval anachronism he encountered on the way to Guam.
His fellow Texan, John B. Connally, then was secretary of
the Navy.

So while John Carver was busily laying plans to revolu-
tionize education in Micronesia, a totally different set of imperatives—of which he seems to have known very little—
were set in motion. Of course, the United Nations report
embarrassed him, too. There was the brand new administration, bursting with vigor and good intentions, being
kicked unexpectedly in the very place for which he was
responsible. He began to demand action.

Goding hurried back to the territory, which from the new
perspective looked even more dismal: hospitals in collaps-
ing Quonsets, thatched schools, equipment melting into
rust. At that point in mid-1961, the 1962 fiscal year was
starting with its budget for the year following. He made a
snap judgment and, feeling brave, cabled Washington that
he wanted to ask Congress for $10 million, though he could
not yet justify the figures. Anything over the $7.5-million
ceiling Congress long since had imposed would require
new enabling legislation. Working with department heads
inherited from the previous administration, Goding put
together his expanded budget. By the time he was ready to
take it to Washington, the total was about $12 million. Since
that was almost double the previous year, Goding was surprised to learn upon arriving that it was all wrong. He was
not doing nearly enough.

"All the key people and especially John Carver were just
appalled at Will's budget," Van Cleve said. "It was the
same old thing, enormous sums for employee housing and
so on and nothing significant for education. There was no
new program thrust. And then they just laid down the law:
no more of that stuff, they told Goding, the initial emphasis
must be on education."

While Goding thrashed about deciding how Micronesians
were to be educated in the future, Interior blithely asked
Congress to take off the spending ceiling. Its rationale was

that since Congress had to approve each year's appropriation, the ceiling was unnecessary. Goding, an older hand in the bureaucracy, knew that would not work. When he returned to Washington, he spoke to Senator Ernest Gruening of Alaska. "Gruening told me, 'We won't remove the ceiling, it's the only hold we have, but we'll raise it.' The senators asked me how much I needed and by that time I was up to $15 million and a week later they passed the bill. The House was tougher and demanded more justification and by the time I had it ready, my need figure was up to $18 million. I went to see Leo O'Brien [Democrat of New York] and he said, 'You know, I don't think we can get the eighteen million. The Senate has already passed fifteen and we'll have no problem with that.' And then he said, I remember, that one senior Republican always wanted to knock off a bite. And he said 'so we'll put it at $17.5 million and give him his bite.' But he didn't bite, as it turned out, so it was reported out at $17.5 million."

It was not what you would call the most careful decision of that year. Later, in conference, House and Senate settled at a $15-million limit for fiscal year 1963, and $17.5 million thereafter.

Despite the casual note, massive charges involving budget increases of 133 percent in a single year do not really happen without sound reasons. The reasons can be traced clearly when one sorts out the realities, but they are complicated because they follow several parallel tracks. One track was that of the Department of Interior, which was essentially humanitarian. Another was strategic and centered in the National Security Council. Another was congressional, which, though very shallow, managed rather neatly to combine the humanitarian and strategic impulses. The humanitarian view, though not basic to the American impulse, was certainly valid, and nowhere was this more clear than among the Americans serving in the Trust Territory.

For these people on their faraway islands, the sudden unsolicited outpouring of money naturally came as a joyous surprise. People who had gone sleepily from day to day as their establishment rusted away found themselves galvanized by the new perception. In their own eyes their duty was redefined in a moment, and suddenly all the past was failure and something quite like a sense of guilt settled over them. "I remember it was quite sudden," an old hand said. "People at meetings would discuss this or that shortcoming and then they would say that it just made them ashamed to be Americans. I didn't like that. I thought it was a lot of crap." But with this new mood there came a huge sense of enthusiasm and urgency. America had dogged it for years, granted—but now they were going to *move*. Under that impulse, of course, the action itself became central and the direction secondary.

The new enthusiasm was evident in the annual reports made by the high commissioner's office. For years those reports had been small, staid documents full of restraint and sober comment. But those written after Goding learned his budgetary prospects seemed to glow with new enthusiasm and brave intention.

Early in 1962, A. M. Rosenthal of *The New York Times* arrived to do a story on the revolution that was to be worked in Micronesia. Read today, the story is strangely gauche; but Rosenthal's naive and unquestioning acceptance of the new assumptions reflects the equally naive momentum that had overtaken the islands. The story was datelined Truk and opened:

> The United States, looking back on fourteen years of trusteeship over the silent, waiting islands of the South Seas, has found its own record meager and wanting and insufficient to its honor.

And it continued in a rush:

> Now, with a mixture of embarrassment for its past and zeal for the future, the administration of the is-

lands of Micronesia . . . is promising that the people of the territory will no longer be treated as stone-age figures in a living museum. . . . a pledge is being made . . . [that] the United States will put more money, more planning and more direction into the islands and will step up the creepingly slow pace of development. . . .

. . . at the beginning of 1962 the assessment is that not enough, by far, has been done and that the United States has not lived up to its own potential in the islands or the potentials and desires of the islanders. This . . . is the assessment of the Americans [here, and of] important officials in Washington. . . .

. . . some important developments are taking place in this territory. . . . There is, to start with, a willingness—an outpouring eagerness—on the part of Americans to look fully and frankly at the United States record in the trusteeship territory and to try to assess it fully and frankly. There are few American officials in the islands, if any, who are satisfied with the record. Many of them say flatly that they are ashamed of it.

Rosenthal went on to quote an unidentified American who he said stopped him to say, "I just want to tell you that I am ashamed to be an American."

Right-thinking Americans were doing good things, however, and the story suggested that it wasn't all that difficult:

. . . across the thirty-five mile wide Truk Lagoon is the island group of Tol. A young American farm specialist found that the islanders were dependent on a trading company in Moen to buy the copra taken from their coconuts and that to this company went a substantial share of the dollar or so a day the islanders earned. Now there is a cooperative on Tol, with its own boat and its own warehouses and its own store. The profits are accumulating pleasantly.*

U.S. officials, Rosenthal found, vehemently told anyone who would listen that they had been kept short of money "with which to do their job well and proudly." They had been silent before, he found, but now "they sense a change in top-level policy and this has opened their own emotional sluice-gates, letting out their pent-up criticisms."

Rosenthal spent a lot of his time on the islands with José Benitez, who was deputy high commissioner and a strangely mercurial figure. Benitez was from Puerto Rico, where he had broken with Democratic powers to become an early supporter of John F. Kennedy. The new administration obligingly found him a job as far from Puerto Rico as possible. If Goding lacked that essential flash, Benitez was overendowed; known everywhere as Pepe, he turned into a sort of supersalesman of things American, roving from island to island and singing his song. In a story that has many variations, Chief Petrus, the grand old man of Truk, is said to have listened to Benitez and then observed (with that succinctness of aphorism that is a Micronesian trait) that Benitez was like a local bird that flew about singing its own name and "comes down to earth once a year and flops its wings and makes a lot of noise and flies away." Goding detested him.

Rosenthal wrote a sidebar on Benitez which seems to sum up the nature of the American conviction in Micronesia and its depth and thoughtfulness. Together they approached a school in Yap which Rosenthal described as a tin shack. Benitez said:

> "My opinion of this school is this!" Then he kicked the walls, which quivered. "A tin shack! This is not a school! This is not America!"

* *The New York Times*, February 12, 1962, p. 1.

The story continued:

A half-hour later the Deputy High Commissioner
was beaming. He was riding on the cab roof of a huge
earthmover clearing the way for a new airstrip. "This,
this is America," he cried happily. "Progress! Bull-
dozers! America!"

When islanders or local officials asked dubiously how he
would pay for the programs he envisioned, Rosenthal
quoted Benitez rather improbably as saying, "Papa, no
more 'How about the money?' That is the way it used to be,
not the way it will be now. Money that is not your job, it is
our job. You tell us what you need and let us go and fight
for the money, for the schools and the hospitals and the
roads. If we fail, then we will have fought for a good thing
and not just sat back and said, 'Where's the money, where's
the money?' These are our brothers! Brothers! Brothers!"*

You could question Benitez's wisdom or his maturity—
but not his goodwill. Back in Washington, Assistant Secretary Carver doubtless was touched with the arrogant assumption of the period that problems were somehow easy
for men who cared, but he did care. "Carver's motives were
humanitarian," Van Cleve said firmly. "Whether White
House support came for other reasons I don't know, but
there is no question about Interior—we were concerned
with the Micronesian people."

But of course, there were other reasons and it is obvious
that they controlled. The basic strategic significance of Micronesia to the United States had not changed; if anything,
it had intensified since World War II. The times were difficult and unstable in 1961 and 1962, after the Bay of Pigs
and before the Cuban missile crisis. The administration was
redrawing American foreign policy, stressing flexibility and
the capacity for response. It had organized the Special

* *Ibid.*

Forces with their flashy green berets. Asia was increasingly volatile and the U.S. footing there, once taken for granted, had become tenuous. The administration was deep in negotiations in Laos. American advisors were going quietly into Vietnam and soon would be told to fire when fired upon. Any dreams of a Nationalist Chinese resurgence from Formosa were fading, and on the mainland, China remained implacably hostile in the wake of the Korean War. The movement to block American use of Okinawa lay ahead, as did increasing reluctance on the parts of Japan and of the Philippines to share in American military affairs. More than ever, in the strategic view it was important to make sure that the U.S. position was secure in those islands that straddled the western Pacific.

Given this new urgency, the old policy of holding fast and ignoring the future seemed old-fashioned, which was not a stance the Kennedy administration admired. There was something incompatible in the American view of itself circa 1961 and the tight military control that required even the governor of Guam to have a security clearance to go to his post. Nor was the control very effective. The Micronesian people were still quiescent, but there were signs of the disaffection that was to come. "It was clear that Radio Peking and Japanese radio was all they listened to," said Michael Forrestal, who then was a special assistant to President Kennedy.

Thus the United States had run Micronesia for its own purpose rather than for the benefit of the Micronesian people, which is one definition of colonialism. Now the United Nations was challenging colonialism and the Kennedy Administration was maneuvering in New York to place itself on the humanitarian side of this suddenly hot issue.

So while Assistant Secretary Carver pressed High Commissioner Goding to restructure Micronesian education, the more significant review of U.S. policy there was going forward at a considerably higher level of government. It involved the Department of State (which dealt with the

United Nations), civilian representatives of the Department of Defense, uniformed military officers, and presidential assistants for foreign policy. When studies were made and positions developed, it went on the agenda of the National Security Council. The National Security Council usually meets in the White House. The President sits in when he chooses. State, Defense, and the uniformed services have regular seats. The Department of Interior is not included.

The National Security Council agreed that it was time to get serious and to bind Micronesia permanently to the United States. It could be a commonwealth or a territory like Guam or even a watery state like Hawaii, but it must become irrevocably American. This meant that a Micronesian plebiscite must be held at some undetermined time in the future, and that the United States must win it. So the policy aimed at ensuring that when plebiscite day arrived, Micronesians would be so impressed with the United States, so pleased with its guidance and excited by its benefits, that they would vote overwhelmingly for a permanent arrangement.

That plebiscite, as it turns out, has yet to be held.

One of the great ironies of the U.S. position in Micronesia is that if it had held the plebiscite at any earlier time the people almost certainly would have voted themselves into the United States. But the harder the United States worked to win Micronesia, the poorer its chances of doing so became; today it is at something like swords' points with all of Micronesia except the Marianas. Presumably the United States took no action when it might have because there was no urgency then, and it was easier to let the situation drift than to risk stirring a reaction at the United Nations.

The new policy was embodied formally in a controlling document known as *National Security Action Memorandum No. 145*, issued in mid-1962 with the highest security classification. It covered a number of points. One was to remove the security lid from the territory. The Central Intelligence Agency's Naval Technical Training Unit would be abandoned. Control of Saipan would move from the Navy to the trust territory government. Entry of foreign nationals and foreign vessels would still be limited, but otherwise the territory would be completely open except for specific military bases.

This opening was symbolic of the larger intentions for the islands. They were to be developed however possible. The economy would be improved. Self-government, with elected district legislatures and a territorial congress, would be advanced. Education, health, and social welfare would be stressed. Transportation would be improved. Water systems, sewer systems, landing strips, hospitals, housing, would be built.

NSAM-145 was secret and remains so today, but its terms have leaked widely. Over the years the well-known existence of this paper—which aims explicitly at influencing a plebiscite—has been cited by Micronesian nationalists who scent conspiracy in the U.S. management of Micronesia. But in fact, it appears that while the United States acted entirely for its own benefit, it nevertheless thought in terms of buying rather than of stealing the place. The key point is that in every formulation, the vote would be free: the intention was to influence it, not to coerce it.

Unfortunately, however, it never was clear how this was to be done, except by exposing the people to American largesse. Meller believes we never had any real goals for the territory, which is why we now say—now that the society is in the soup—that after all, it really is up to the Micronesians to decide their own destiny, that any stirring around on our part would be colonialist. Robert Mangan, Carver's deputy, thought the successful plebiscite was the whole point and that no one looked beyond that. But if in the recesses of the Pentagon it occurred to someone that Micronesians might acquire a taste for a life they could not afford on their own, well, that would not be inconsistent. Indeed, intentional or otherwise, that may be the real reason that no realistic policy for the future ever appeared.

It is clear, at any rate, that what the people on the islands saw as radical change actually was only a tactical shift. The strategic view and intention were unaltered.

The Congressional view, though no better informed than today (and a somewhat bemused combination of strategy and humanitarianism), was neatly summarized in a wandering discourse by James G. Fulton, a Pennsylvania Republican. "I look forward to the time when this area will be a state of the United States," he told the House in 1962. "These are peace-loving good people who, with education, can have the same abilities we do. If they are given adequate technical training they can become a very fine anchor and backup in depth for the free world just east of the Philippine Islands. We in the United States should never forget that this gives us the backup of three million square miles of islands and of friendly people who have caused no trouble whatever in the Pacific. These people are a wonderful law-abiding people and it was a privilege for many of us World War II servicemen to take part in their liberation and the restoration of their human rights and freedom." They should be developed, he explained, so they could become strong, "not only for the defense of the United States and the Pacific area, but for their own good."*

The recipients of all this, the Micronesians themselves, were hardly consulted. They were treated as a passive screen on which the great plans of the controlling power would be cast in full color. And generally, they seemed to accept the role at the time. "The mood was from above, strictly from above," Van Cleve said, "not from the indigens. Of course they would have caught up, but they hadn't then."

Micronesians had been passive under the Japanese and they remained so for two decades under the Americans. The chief complaints had been the lack of economic development and the use of their islands as test sites in the 1950s

* *Congressional Record*, July 2, 1962.

for American atomic and hydrogen weapons, and these always were tentative and muted. From this point onward, as they also responded to change, they became increasingly restless and more and more insistent on taking their future into their own hands. At the time, however, though they expressed some cynical doubt that much actually would happen, they seemed content with the American view that more was better. It was assumed, after all, that the new policies would lead to economic development, and generally they were willing to wait and see.

NSAM-145 stated goals, not means. But its stress on development was consistent with the plans Carver and Mangan already were implementing. They had asked High Commissioner Goding to put the weight of his program on education, and President Kennedy's message, on signing the legislation that more than doubled the Trust Territory budget ceiling, ratified their decision. The statement that the new program would "place great emphasis on education [which] is the key to all further progress," with the intention of "striking improvement . . . upgrading education to a level comparable to the level which has been taken for granted in the United States for decades," was startlingly specific. Considering the state of Micronesian education, it was a huge projection.

Thus education became the chosen vehicle of change and of U.S. strategic policy.

None of the people who designed the program to carry out Kennedy's instructions was experienced in Micronesia. Carver and Mangan had been there once. Goding was a newcomer. He and Robert Gibson, the territory's education director (who certainly knew the most about the reality of education in the islands), fell out immediately. Gibson had Democratic connections and apparently had hoped for the high commissioner's post for himself. As he listened to the plans for change, he began to take violent exception.

By this time, partly at the insistence of the House, a so-

called task force on Micronesia, with middle-level membership from Interior, Defense, and State, had been formed.
The new program was worked out in conjunction with the
task force; thereafter Goding's annual reports always described the "complete reevaluation" made in 1962 of the territory's educational needs.

The new concept had three main elements. The first called
for universal high-school education in Micronesia. This
meant abandoning the Pacific Islands Central School with
its democratizing and unifying effect. A high school would
be opened in each district center by adding one grade per
year to intermediate schools. PICS—to retain its acronym—
would become Ponape Island Central School, but thereafter
it enrolled only Ponapeans and was just another high
school.

The new high schools necessarily were boarding schools,
since most students still came from the outer islands. Boarding schools are expensive, so despite the new budget plans,
the high schools soon became financial burdens. As a result, Goding said later, it was necessary to make them almost entirely academic institutions. Vocational education is
expensive. It also is difficult to organize quickly, and suddenly time seemed the most critical element of all.

Schools assembled in a hurry are likely to be standard
models. These new high schools were right out of the
United States. They lacked even the self-governing factor
and the agriculture and shop which had distinguished
PICS, which itself was an academic model.

Thus quite suddenly the territory began advertising the
right of every youngster to an education through the twelfth
grade in an academic, college-oriented school, despite the
fact that the society producing the children had little use for
more than a handful of college graduates. For several years
circumstances managed to obscure the penalties of this
move, but they now are becoming clear.

At the same time, the new move suddenly offered to everyone what before had been reserved for the elite—intellectual or otherwise—that had gone to PICS. Under the old system, only the special or lucky went on, and the rest fitted into life as it was. Now every parent could expect—indeed, insist upon—advanced education for his child. In fact, universal high school has not been achieved to this day; the high schools still cannot accommodate the outpouring of students from the elementary schools. But the pressure that was set in motion in 1962 has been growing ever since.

The most immediate and dramatic element of the new program (though in the end it was less important than the shift to universal high schools) was the decision to take over elementary schools and to fund them directly. Even today, Goding sees this radical shift of funds as the basic change. Local responsibility for schools was dropped, and the territorial government began a furious building campaign. Those little thatched schools open to the weather—that had so shocked the visitors from Washington—began to disappear. Some educators tried to replace them with larger schools using the same indigenous materials, but the Micronesians, peering bemusedly into the flowing end of the new cornucopia, suddenly exerted their weight and demanded cinderblock buildings which would also serve as typhoon shelters.

In the first year of the program, 234 elementary classrooms were to be built; eventually the figure went beyond 600. Each classroom was to be properly equipped for school in the American sense. One of the results of this change was to lift schools far beyond the capacity of the village or outer island on which they were located to have any part in them. Local character vanished as local support ended. The vast psychological support that local interest had implied also went, and schools have been having trouble with communities ever since. Today, this reversal of attitude has progressed so far that schools have started hiring guards to protect against vandalism. Another result was that the teachers who had functioned, if sometimes barely, in those old thatched schools now were seen as increasingly inadequate.

That led directly to the third major element of the new program, the decision to abandon teaching in the vernacular and to make English the language of instruction from the moment the child entered school. This was totally a Washington idea. "Someone had the guts," Mangan said, "to see if the old wives' tales from the anthropologists about the people not wanting to learn in English were true. Well, we found the people wanted to learn English and almost overnight we decided we would solve the problem of all those miserable little mimeographed native texts through the fourth grade."

Out in the territory, the education director, Robert Gibson, was scandalized and outraged. He believed in the virtues of vernacular teaching. "It just blasts a kid's perception of his own culture to force him to start school, a fantastic new process for him anyway, in a totally new language. That's all the more true when the school itself is oriented to a culture totally different than his own, I always believed that," Gibson said. It happens that the weight of opinion among modern linguists is firmly on his side.

Goding, of course, made no pretense to being an educator. Yet his reflection today, a decade-and-a-half later, suggests the range of ignorance territorial leaders brought to the subject. "Teaching English shouldn't undermine their culture. I felt Bob was overemphasizing the problem. They were very unlikely to forget their own language."

At first Gibson assumed that the new plans for English instruction were just another high-flown Washington scheme. For after all, as he quickly explained to Goding and to anyone else who would listen, Micronesian teachers really couldn't teach English because most of them couldn't speak English. Some years earlier an American had had a graphic illustration of this: in a Micronesian classroom he had found chalked on a blackboard the teacher's version, taken phonetically, of *My Country 'tis of Thee:*

> Mai kantri ti op ti
> Suit lant op liperti
> Op ti ai sin
> Lant op ti Pilkrims prait
> Lant wer mai paters dait
> Prom eperi mauntin sait
> Let pretum rin.*

Gibson was sure that teacher inability would cancel the ill-conceived order to teach everything in English. Instead it led to a crash program to give Micronesian teachers adequate English. Each district set up training programs. Headquarters hired a linguist to improve language training. The Micronesian Teacher Education Center was established on the PICS campus at Ponape; eventually it became the Community College of Micronesia, which functions rather haphazardly today. But most important of all, the pressure for English led to the decision to bring out a large contingent of American teachers to take over classrooms in Micronesia. That would solve the problem of instruction in English, though learning in English might be another question. Goding hoped to persuade the Peace Corps to send teachers to Micronesia; but when Sargent Shriver refused, the territory decided to import regular American classroom teachers and to hire them on a standard contract.

"I thought English was critical," Mangan said. "They couldn't hope for unity without a universal language." And, revealing the underlying American assumption that college naturally follows lower education, he added, "There

---

* Quoted in Elizabeth Kelley Antilla, "A History of the People of The Trust Territory of the Pacific Islands and Their Education," doctoral dissertation, University of Texas, 1965.

was no way they could go on to further training in Hawaii
or the United States without a much better capacity in English then Micronesian teachers could give them."

Importing teachers posed new problems. First, they had
to be found. Most were recruited by newspaper ads right
out of classrooms in the western United States. They were
shipped out raw, with no special training and certainly
with no language training, because now there was great
hurry to get the new program moving. At the same time,
the expected arrival of American teachers put additional
pressure on shifting the whole school system to English.
Otherwise the new teachers would be as baffled as the students they were to teach, and the whole brilliant idea might
collapse.

Since the circumstances of Micronesia are rude, and the
new teachers were not of the self-sacrificing Peace Corps
mold, it was obvious the Trust Territory would have to
house them. The result was a totally new construction program. A new teacher's house was scheduled for every
school, with 104 planned the first year for 140 teachers. The
expenses of the new program already were beginning to
exceed the expanded budget. This would happen again and
again, so that while money boomed through Micronesia, al-
tering the society as it went, the people handling it universally felt that they had too little to accomplish what was
before them. This may be the reason that they always saw
themselves as poor instead of newly rich, and why so few of
them questioned the wisdom of what their money bought.
It became rooted in their minds that they spent too little. All
these steps were taken with little thought. No one asked
why education should be the centerpiece of the new thrust.
"I wouldn't say we moved with any philosophically
thought-out plan," Goding said.

Ruth Van Cleve remembers that education was considered appropriate without any question. It was good *per se*,
it was our moral duty. Carver, the man behind the whole
idea, simply feels that anything that limits education limits

the development of human potential, and that such limitation is inconsistent with American ideals.

Mangan also rejects challenges to the basic assumptions, and he has described Carver in quintessential New Frontier terms: "Carver's not the kind of guy who asks a lot of questions. If it's a good idea he does it."

But as usual in Micronesia, there is more to the question than idealism or even good ideas. Probably the fact that the United Nations visiting mission in 1961 had complimented the administration for its universal elementary schools served as a guide—educational development certainly would be acceptable to the critics in the tower on the East River. But even more important, the administration was in a hurry, and education is an easy place to show quick gains. Education also is easily quantifiable—books, schools, numbers of teachers, numbers of graduates, can be made to add up to progress. At the same time, it is not very accountable. There are no inconvenient indicators—like the death rates that plague health administrators. If an educator's statistics ring strong, it will be years before anyone will know how well it all worked, and by then he will have moved on to higher posts on the basis of his presumed successes. Furthermore, education is easy to sell, especially to American congressmen; it has a heartfelt ring that comforts them.

Education was politically useful in the territory. It touched most people, demonstrated concern for their children (and thus for them), and created a cadre of Micronesian teachers. Spread ubiquitously through the islands, the teachers served as an obviously stabilizing effect, since they were interested above all in maintaining their positions in the status quo. And American education certainly imposed an ideological link to the United States, conditioning both teachers and students to a similar world view. Young Micronesians now are rejecting American dominance, but they probably do so from an American mindset.

So the answer to the question, why education instead of economic development, is that education was easy, quick, visible, and useful, while economic development was and is hard and slow. And it also is true that successful economic development would have made Micronesians independent, which is not what the United States wanted; education, as it has turned out, has made them more rather than less dependent.

Military control of the Trust Territory ended July 1, 1962, by executive order, and the territorial headquarters moved into the old CIA base atop the highest mountain on Saipan. It was a hectic time. Goding made thirty-eight trips to Washington in the first four years, and the quip was coined, "In Goding we trust." Yet he never could satisfy the pressure in Washington, where he was seen as inept and as a failure. Part of the problem was the terrible distance that separated the islands he ruled. All construction materials had to be shipped in and rarely arrived in sequence. Work was approached with island torpor and accomplishment deadlines came and went without effect. Everything, Washington complained, seemed to take forever.

Goding was not a creative man and had little flair. He was both cautious and stubborn, which made his decisions slow. "He could spend days on a fifteen-minute decision," a subordinate said later. In Washington's eyes, he was further damaged by the comparison with Rex Lee, a much more energetic type who was governor of American Samoa. Why can't Goding be like Lee, people asked. In time the carping pressure began to wear Goding down. The tone of his annual reports is interesting. The 1962 report, written in the middle of that year, seems to see the new surge somewhat hesitantly. The 1963 report is exuberant, full of optimism, plans, confidence, expectations. The 1964 report, though it assures the reader that all goes forward on schedule, takes on a reserved, cautious, almost somber note, as if the administration that produced it is bruised and tired. Goding seems to have been inextricably caught between the dreams of Washington and the slow, difficult, implacable reality of the islands.

He also was caught in the inconsistencies of the situation. Robert Gibson, then with much more than a decade as the territory's education director, believed that the Washington-mandated change was a critical mistake and that it flowed from questionable motives. Once an assistant secretary, presumably Carver, asked him how he would prefer to spend the money newly available—money marked for American teachers and for their new houses. Gibson said he would spend it on training Micronesian teachers, and quotes the reply, "But that will take too long. We don't have time for that." Another official told him that teaching English was of paramount importance to prepare Micronesians for "finally becoming American citizens."

Washington saw Gibson's resistance in the starkest terms. "Right after the war," Mangan said, "the Navy brought in the anthropologists, and they never lost their foothold. Their attitude was that the only important thing was the preservation of culture and that the way to do that was to maintain the islands as a sort of living museum. I called it a living zoo. So the battle was between the preservationists and the modernists without very much attempt to weld them together."

This conflict was summed up in the pejorative phrase, "the zoo theory," coined, Lola Smith said, "by some nitwit in Washington." It was never used during the time which it describes, the 1950s. Dirk Ballendorf thinks that the attitude then was not even social, as the term now is used, but economic. The idea was that it was a mistake to build the islands, educationally and otherwise, faster than the supporting economy was built. The dark side of that approach, however, was that in practice neither the economy nor anything else was developed. There was no positive approach to the future; indeed, there was no approach at all. The islands were stagnant, which created an inevitable vacuum as time passed. Obviously something would have filled that vacuum eventually; as it happened, the thrust of the New Frontier did so, its practitioners coining the zoo theory concept to explain the past. The stagnation of the 1950s was not workable, but neither was its replacement. Carl Heine, now an angry nationalist and the author of *Micronesia at the Crossroads*, the first book by a Micronesian, believes that whatever the intent of the Kennedy-administration policies, their effect was "to destroy the Micronesian's chance to depend on himself, to take his rightful place in his own society."

In the summer of 1962 there was a small outbreak of polio in the Marshalls. Polio vaccine had been discovered a decade earlier but it had never come to Micronesia, partly because health officials were uneasy about the effect of inoculating a society that had never been touched by the disease. So they waited until the disease arrived in force, carried by American children at Kwajalein, and several deaths and some crippling followed.

President Kennedy learned of the epidemic the following December and exploded. One can imagine his concern. It was official (if still secret) U.S. policy to persuade Micronesians that their best interests lay with America, and the first thing that happened was an epidemic that seemed eaily preventable. The United Nations had attacked the U.S. administration again in 1962 for its Micronesian shortcomings, and now this would have to be explained. Kennedy had more than doubled the budget, proclaimed education as the keystone of a new advance, and told Interior to get on with it. His next awareness of Micronesia was this new disaster.

Kennedy called in one of his aides, Michael Forrestal. "This polio thing had come to the attention of the President," Forrestal said, "and he started asking what was going on, how could this have happened? He asked a lot of questions—he was angry—and we began finding out what was happening. The more he learned, the more upset he got."

Like any executive, Kennedy did not tell his assistant all of his concerns. "I remember him saying something like,

'How can the United States be what it thinks it is—believes it is—and allow such neglect?' " Forrestal said. Kennedy told Forrestal to go see for himself what was happening in Micronesia. Forrestal did and was shocked, another of the endless line of startled visitors. He came home predictably outraged. Kennedy listened, Forrestal remembered, "and the President said, 'Well, we have to increase the appropriations there at least to the level of Westchester County,' or some such crack. And he said to find a fellow who could take a hard look out there and see what could be done."

Thus was born the famous—or infamous—Solomon Commission, issuer of the Solomon Report, which has become the subject of more myth and folklore than any other single aspect of the American administration of Micronesia. In time the wealth of change that America imposed on Micronesia came to be attributed to the report; in fact the report grew from the pressure for change, not vice versa, a point which Anthony Solomon understood from the beginning.

Solomon is intelligent, capable, acerbic, and easily bored, with a low tolerance for fools. Since there are a good many of these around, he is not entirely popular. He made a fortune in business in New York and Mexico City, sold out when it became boring, taught for a year at the Harvard Business School, found academic finance dull, and was ready when the Kennedy administration asked him to head an economic mission to Bolivia. He had just completed this assignment successfully when Forrestal began looking for someone to examine Micronesia. Later Solomon became an assistant secretary of state; today he lives on a farm on the outskirts of Washington and describes himself as a full-time sculptor.

Forrestal felt the main need in Micronesia was economic and was attracted by Solomon's background. A Bureau of the Budget official phoned Solomon, who remembers he had never heard of the islands. "And I asked, do they include the Solomon Islands? [Which, of course, they don't.] And this fellow said he thought so, and I said, 'I can't resist landing on the Solomon Islands and spreading my arms to the natives and saying, *I have returned.*' "

Solomon did not see Kennedy before the mission. He reported to the White House for a briefing by Forrestal, MacGeorge Bundy, and others. "They said that it was so bad out there that they assumed more money would have to be spent, but the question was how? And they also wanted better marks from the people and from the United Nations. They kept getting criticized to the effect that things were worse in Micronesia than they had been under the Japanese."

He was asked to accept as a given the military significance of the islands. "Beyond that, there were two basic premises. First, we had a humanitarian interest and a political self-interest, which included avoiding so much United Nations criticism. Second, eventually we would have to face up to the question of the future and the Pentagon's interest in denying Micronesia to other powers. That was it—there was no other pressure and no other instructions."

Solomon chose eight specialists in economics, agriculture, health, education, and other fields. "The President wanted me to go in June, but I had chartered a sailing vessel in the Greek islands for June." The mission went to Micronesia in July 1963, and stayed about six weeks. Predictably Solomon and Goding disagreed on policy and disliked each other. The mission's report ran six hundred pages in three volumes and was classified. The first volume dealt with the political future and was so sensitive, Solomon says, that the State Department allowed only ten copies to be printed. The other volumes, dealing with social and economic recommendations, eventually were declassified, with political material excised.

Solomon reported to the President on October 9, 1963. Kennedy had read and digested the twenty-page introduction and summary and asked sharp questions. Udall, Carver, and Forrestal sat in on the meeting. "I explained my proposals," Solomon said, "and the President finally said,

'It sounds exactly right, and it seems the unanimous view except for Goding.' Then he turned to Udall and said, 'I want this implemented from A to Z.' " The Solomon Report thus became official U.S. policy, so ordered by another National Security Action Memorandum. But after Kennedy's death, the specifics of the report drifted into limbo. President Johnson was interested enough in Micronesia, but not in Solomon's effort.

Yet the report's reputation has been growing ever since. The mythology about it takes two forms—that it advocated a rigged plebiscite and that it inspired the growth of the 1960s. Actually, it did neither.

The idea that a rigged plebiscite is part of U.S. policy has a real lure for today's angry nationalists in Micronesia, who point to the report's continuing secrecy as proof. But probably the classification is only to cover the embarrassment of some very frank political talk, for the report was predicated on binding Micronesia to the United States at a time when, under the trustreeship agreement, the United States was supposed to be promoting Micronesian self-government. But there is no indication that its methods went beyond persuasion.

In 1971 what purported to be the introduction that Kennedy read that day leaked and was published in a small Micronesian weekly. Donald F. McHenry's recent study* reproduces it, and a careful reading seems to bear out Solomon when he remarks today, "What I understood when I went out, and from Kennedy's response when I returned, was just that you had to be forthcoming on funds, you had to administer well, you had to establish a fair system of self-government, if you wanted to get them to vote for some sort of association with the United States when the plebiscite came. But rigged? Well, of course, if by structuring the alternatives and choosing the timing you are rigging—no,

* Donald F. McHenry, *Micronesia: Trust Betrayed* (Washington, D. C.: Carnegie Endowment for International Peace, 1975), p. 231.

rigging is much too strong. We wanted to influence the outcome of the vote, but that's the nature of any election. The
point is, I always assumed it would be an honest election. It
would be supervised by the United Nations."

The idea that the report inspired the growth of the 1960s
clearly is wrong. Goding believes that in real terms the report soon was forgotten and had little or no effect. Some of
what it recommended in social fields has been done and
some has not. Most of what has happened was in motion
before Solomon ever heard of Micronesia. The Congress of
Micronesia, for example, was formulated in October 1962, at
the first meeting of the territory-wide, appointed Council of
Micronesia. This, with the thrust in education, had grown
from the fertile minds of Carver and Mangan. The economic
development which the report urged, rather blithely ignoring the difficulties, has been largely ignored.

Carver probably sees Solomon's significance most accurately. "Much of what he found we told him before he
ever left Washington," he said. "Solomon's real impact was
as an independent voice."

The report certified and made permanent what Interior
had started almost on impulse and what the President had
expanded with his budget message putting the weight of
the new thrust on education. Even though the succeeding
president lost interest in the report, the momentum it gave
policy continues to this day.

The real reason for the misconception that the report orig-
inated the policy is that affairs ran so slowly in the Trust
Territory that the tremendous changes instituted more than
a year before Solomon appeared did not actually show up in
the islands until 1964, long after the report was made. When
things finally began to happen, the misattribution was natural.

Even the recruiting of American teachers did not actually
begin until September 1963, when Solomon was home writing his report; it was the following year before the first contingent arrived. This hiring was most haphazard. The re-

cruiter interviewed teachers in a hotel and showed them colored pictures, which were much stronger on the islands' beauty than on their isolation. He tried to explain the hardships, but there really is no way to convey the experience of the rude living conditions on an outer island and the psychological impact of being severed from the outside world for weeks at time.

In the hurry there was little screening. Many of those applying were fleeing problems of job or marriage or personality and hoping for a new start in an island paradise. One was a former wrestler who eventually was sent home for abusing children, and many were unstable personalities. The alluring isolation of an island actually is the worst condition for such people: witness the incidence of alcoholism, divorce, and violence in most isolated places.

The instructions given the new teachers did not go far beyond what clothing to bring. Don Topping, now head of the Pacific and Asian Language Institute at the University of Hawaii (which is preparing orthographies in the Micronesian languages), proposed a training course in Hawaii to give the new teachers a sense of Micronesian culture, problems, and most important, language. But the territorial government, prodded constantly by Washington for results, was getting frantic and ruled there was no time for this simple step. Instead Topping went out to the islands and gave the incoming teachers a week-long course on the problems of teaching students of another culture who did not speak English.

The teacher attrition rate was high from the beginning which put continual pressure on recruiting replacements. Some teachers took one look and went home. Most settled in for a year, but resisted leaving the district centers. There, in the larger schools, many of them became simply teachers of English, with Micronesian teachers continuing to carry the rest of the load. No one was very happy. Micronesian teachers were drawing $50 a month, much less than the Americans, and were angered by the houses supplied the newcomers. At the same time, they feared losing their jobs, while the Micronesian communities seemed to feel they already had lost their schools. Now the schools were seen as belonging to the Americans. "Then came the attitude that the government is responsible for all this," said Tarkong Pedro of Palau, chairman of the House Education Committee, Congress of Micronesia, "and when you asked them to work on the schools, they wanted to be paid. It no longer was a community responsibility." The American teachers, on the other hand, in the midst of all their other distresses were miffed because the houses provided them were smaller than the standard houses supplied Americans working for the Trust Territory government.

The schools were expanding so rapidly that it is doubtful that the new teachers actually displaced any Micronesian teachers. In addition to creating new high schools, the system also increased elementary schools from six to eight grades. Since little communication was possible between the Micronesians—teachers and students—on the one hand, and the administration and the new teachers on the other, confusion continued to reign.

The basic curriculum, however, changed very little. It remained an academic system, oriented more than ever to the quite invalid assumption of college as the students' future. Most instruction actually continued in the vernacular since Micronesian teachers had not mastered English (nor have they today). One new and unfortunate feature was that the territory stopped mimeographing vernacular reading material and bought new books in English, which often lay in warehouses since neither teachers nor students could read them. This clumsy dichotomy between hope and fact would hold until 1967 when, with American teachers deserting in droves, the administration bowed to reality and introduced a new program designed to teach English as a second language. The manuals of the day, however, still bravely stated the old intention, still using the future tense, "English shall become the general language for communication and in-

struction in the Trust Territory." Signs went up in
classrooms exhorting students: "Speak English!" Assistant
Secretary Carver remembers walking into a Micronesian
classroom, noticing the sign, and then seeing chalked on
the blackboard the practice sentence: "Take me to the
benjo." The word is Japanese for an overwater privy.

In the midst of waste, confusion, and stunning cultural
arrogance, Washington's educational policies for Micronesia
were being implemented. Robert Gibson's years as director
of education were coming to an end. He had lost his fight
for the old ways. By the fall of 1964 he was inundated in
new teachers and new plans and rude attacks on the culture-oriented concepts in which he believed. Reflecting
sadly on what might have been done over the years with
this cataract of money, he resigned and entered retirement
in Honolulu.

The new construction program crashed along, careening,
colliding with the reality of the islands, but gaining. The
building of those houses that miffed the new teachers
seemed miraculous to those who knew what was involved.
The logistical problems of bringing the right quantities of
the right materials in the right order to the right place to
maintain steady construction on islands thousands of miles
apart were overwhelming. "First place," said Tom Gilliland,
who was on Goding's staff at the time, "it took months, literally months, to get supplies. So we often had to order
things in general, before we knew what the actual require-
ments would be, and then we had to use them no matter
what. But if we waited until we knew exact specifications,
we'd lose another year's construction time. Some of the materials arrived late and we still had delays, and others arrived long before they were needed, and then we had
storage and pilferage problems. Once some two hundred
thousand dollars' worth of lumber arrived just at the start of
the rainy season. We couldn't move it and we had to store it
out of doors, so we asked permission to use some of the
lumber to build sheds to protect the rest. And we were

turned down, just some bureaucratic snarl, you know, but we lost three quarters of the lumber. But that was the exception—usually the problem was that we were desperately short of supplies. I remember sending boxes of pencils to the carpentry shop to be cut in half so all the kids in a school could have pencils."

School building—the new high schools, elementaries, teacher housing—was the major construction, but money was pouring in and all branches of government were starting new programs. One effect of this was that the territory began to take on a somewhat false look of prosperity. Roads leading to all those new buildings were improved, though few were paved. Docking facilities were expanded. Work began on landing strips for the territory's recently acquired DC-4s. Skilled labor was imported, as it is generally today, but local people were used for unskilled labor, and many thus entered a cash economy for the first time and began acquiring the tastes that accompany cash. Much of their work was gathering sand for cement, often from the nearest lagoon. Ever afterwards buildings made from this cement would leach salt, which is one reason that it still is almost impossible to keep buildings painted in the Trust Territory.

Drooling salt is the least of the buildings' problems, however, for the haste of that period produced a series of small disasters well described by Ruth Van Cleve in testimony before a House subcommittee in 1967:

> . . . the pressures have been so acute that the administrators in the trust territories, starting with the first moment of the accelerated program in 1963, felt that it was more important to do something, even if it was not the perfect thing, in a hurry. The consequences are in many instances very unfortunate. We have schools without plumbing, schools without water, schools without electricity because we did not pause to decide how the electric lines should be run, or to resolve in some instances very acute water prob-

lems. There is good question now as to whether this was a sensible way to proceed.

The fact is that some three hundred classrooms were constructed on what now appears to be a very haphazard basis. We have certainly now concluded that we must pause and look again.*

Building was as costly and wasteful as it is today, always taking more money than anyone had expected. Most construction was too far from headquarters to be supervised and was perforce left in the hands of people who were anything but professional builders. Every job was subject to pilferage and substitution of materials and fraud. Yet initiative and imaginative use of local materials was blocked by strict regulations and a narrow and essentially frightened bureaucratic view. Those buildings that were supposed to impress the Micronesians seemed always to leach salt or to rust. Their glass louvres soon were replaced with plywood; their wallboard mildewed and curled in the damp; their wiring threw sparks; their slab floors cracked; their roofs leaked in the violent rainstorms.

In 1966 a new American event gave Micronesian perceptions another rattling. The Peace Corps arrived. High Commissioner Goding had sought Peace Corps help at the beginning and had been refused, but that changed when Solomon recommended the use of volunteers to produce quick change. The Corps came in force—some nine hundred volunteers at its peak, one for every ninety Micronesians at the time, the highest per capita Peace Corps program in the world. There were three volunteers for every American in the Trust Territory government.

There was immediate antagonism between the newcomers and the old hands, and neither side handled itself

* U.S. Congress, House of Representatives, Committee on Appropriations, *Hearings before a Subcommittee: Department of the Interior and Related Agencies Appropriations for 1968* (Washington D.C.: Government Printing Office, 1967), p. 1052.

well. Dirk A. Ballendorf, the leading authority on the Peace Corps in Micronesia, where he himself served, notes that the volunteers were openly contemptuous of the regulars and expected to set things right immediately. He cites a memorandum of the day that announces with rather breathtaking gall that the Corps "intends to alter substantially in a relatively short period of time, say three to five years, the twenty-year record of neglect and dismal achievement" of the Department of Interior. The fault, of course, was not with the newcomers' assessment, but with their expectations.

Some three hundred of the volunteers were teachers, and many were posted to outer islands, where some were the first Americans the people had ever known. Symbolic of the change and awakening this produced was the matter of the air/sea rescue teams. Volunteers arrived at their islands with radios. When they found illness and injury they viewed it from a western technological perspective and radioed for professional help. Presumably there always had been illness and injury; the new ingredient was the American with radio. But once he requested help, the Navy was obliged to send an aircraft. The Navy resented this and eventually abandoned the entire service. But the medical question was the least of it, for the situation certainly had a powerful effect on the Micronesians' view of the whole situation and of its potentials. If you could talk to the American, and he could summon a four-engine aircraft from five hundred miles away. . . .

Ballendorf notes that the Micronesians quickly learned to exploit the situation. At the same time, many volunteers, moving into a perceived vacuum, began expanding their role from teacher to social activist. They expanded the Micronesian grasp of English, but much more important, they expanded the Micronesian understanding of how the system worked and what rights it gave individuals. Peace Corps lawyers began assisting the Congress of Micronesia, which more and more placed itself in the role of adversary

to the Trust Territory government. Many outer-island volunteers became advocates of the people of their islands
against the territorial government. On Kili Island, volunteers helped the people prepare a petition to the United Nations demanding the return of their home island of Bikini,
which had been taken for atomic tests and was still held. It
is hard to imagine a more justifiable move—or one more
alarming to the bureaucratically narrow men whose responsibility it all was. Soon various petitions and legal actions
were underway and the territory was scrambling to explain
itself against what it now perceived as a new enemy. The
volunteers, Ballendorf notes, were not federal employees
and were free to criticize. But territorial officials tended to
see the Peace Corps as just another arm of government, and
hence took its attacks quite personally. Even today, John
Carver's face darkens when the Peace Corps is mentioned.
"Micronesia," he snapped, "is the most unworthy page in
Peace Corps history."

Part of the problem was the anomalous fact that Micronesia was not a foreign country, but it suffered from many of
the problems of underdeveloped countries. Fresh from
growing social activism in the United States and idealistic
almost by definition, the inexperienced young volunteers
found it intolerable that their own government should be
supporting the very conditions they were organized to alle-
viate in other countries. Yet as Ballendorf notes, in the end
their efforts were counter-productive. They were, as he put
it, "energetic amateurs," often callow and naive, much
stronger on indignation than on the difficult question of
solutions. One of their most powerful effects was to raise
expectations among Micronesians that they had no capacity
to satisfy.

But probably the more accurate view is that they were
simply actors in a much longer story, catalysts of an attitude
among Micronesians that was growing anyway and that
was the inevitable result of American management since
World War II. Stirred by education, changed by the insertion of relatively huge sums of money into their lives, the

Micronesians were moving into the world and beginning to consider their own interests, and at most the volunteers probably did no more than hurry the process slightly. And maybe they were right all along, for from the beginning of their experience, they perceived Micronesians as an oppressed, colonialized people, and gradually that is how the Micronesians have come to see themselves.

Yet while the money controlled by the territory's officers was making such change and stirring up the beginnings of animosity, those officers themselves remained under fearful pressure from Washington to do more. The problem was a combination of big dreams and bad management. There were few mechanisms to control what happened once a program was set in motion, let alone to limit its cost or to coordinate its cost with other costs. Everyone dreamed big—or big enough, they hoped, to satisfy their critics in Washington—and then the programs soared right through the territory's spending requests and left it broke again. The irony was that they had started the decade with small budgets, scrimping and cutting corners. Budgets had soared, plans had followed, and here they were scrimping and cutting corners again. The budget messages after 1963 had a somber, harassed sound.

The ceiling on spending was lifted and lifted again to pour more money into producing what people in Washington seemed to feel could easily be a Micronesian renaissance—if the right man just could be found to direct it. And Goding, the Washington group long since had decided, was not at all the right man. Almost from the start there had been persistent attempts to fire him, which Goding had fought off with his own political weight. Once Senator Bartlett of Alaska had spoken directly to President Kennedy to save Goding. But gradually the scar tissue accumulated, Goding tired, and by 1966 nothing could save him. The final explosion came over some trifle between Goding and Udall, but the real problem was the weight of those angry years. Udall told Goding to pack and be gone in a week.

In 1967, with a new high commissioner installed, there

was another surge of growth in Micronesia, a gain inspired from Washington. Another White House assistant came out, was predictably shocked, and went home to write another angry memo. He was almost ashamed to be an American and he recommended vigorous spending on all fronts to eliminate this and that failure. The budget ceilings went up and the new high commissioner, William Norwood, remembers now that the money came in faster than he could find projects to spend it on.

All the change in Micronesia grew from money. Money built the schools and hired the teachers and laid the roads and changed the transport and offered wages and drew people into the district centers and gave them a new sense of their own worth and of the possibilities of the world. And so startling is the sense of money-change itself that it is worth examining the Trust Territory budgets over the years in tabular form. There are various ways to calculate the budgets, and the figures used here include the small local income. In the early period, local income produce a considerable portion of the total budget; toward the end it produced less than five percent, even though tax-based local income itself had grown sharply. This, then, with minor variations, is a picture of the growth in spending in the Trust Territory of the Pacific Islands across the period:

1961—$ 7.4 million
1962—$ 7.9 million
1963—$16.7 million
1964—$22.1 million
1965—$23.5 million
1966—$23.7 million
1967—$25.9 million
1968—$35.3 million
1969—$41.2 million
1970—$52.9 million
1971—$62.9 million
1972—$73.6 million
1973—$79.6 million
1974—$80.0 million

This surge of money made an indelible impression on the people of Micronesia and on their attitudes toward themselves, toward Americans, and toward their future. It did not change the islands much physically, especially since the construction budgets began to level off in the later years as the operations budgets grew. The islands today have the same look of dilapidated decay that shocked Carver and Solomon and all the other Americans who have gone there and come home dismayed and anxious for improvements.

But what did change was the relationship of Micronesians to the economy. The building projects demanded labor. Additional schools, expanded public works, new docks and water systems and power plants, meant people to man them. The intensely bureaucratic nature of the Trust Territory, exacerbated by the great distances between districts (making each like a separate country), made many more clerks necessary. Typing, bookkeeping, and drawing up reports and statements became important new occupations. And the employment rolls of the territory grew and grew. Again the sense of that growth is best given in tabular figures. The figures include Americans, but even at the beginning they made only ten percent of the total and now make considerably less. The remainder are Micronesians. Like all Micronesian figures, these vary, but they are drawn from official records and give an accurate sense of the trend:

> 1962—2,686
> 1963—4,017
> 1964—4,437
> 1965—5,083
> 1966—5,078
> 1967—5,235
> 1968—5,360
> 1969—5,630
> 1970—7,835
> 1971—8,770
> 1972—9,022
> 1973—7,736
> 1974—6,815

While the last two figures exclude the employment of Micronesians by the military at Kwajalein and elsewhere, it also is true that rising costs have led to a curtailment of employment, which is the key to much of the unrest now assailing the islands.

This doubling and redoubling of employment among a small population had a startling effect on the perceptions of the Micronesian people. It inserted cash into the lives of many people who had lived until then on a subsistence basis. It started the flow of people to the district centers, where the jobs were and where subsistence living is not really possible. And it fixed among Micronesians a perception that seems not to have faltered to this day—that education equals success and success equals a government job.

For the new hiring put a high premium on anyone who could speak even a little English and who had some understanding of how a western social system worked. The folk knowledge slowly gained in the villages by the leaders of a static society had no value in this new situation. Instead the jobs and the money went to youngsters who had had been to school. A diploma from PICS, to say nothing of time spent in college abroad, was a guarantee of a good job and a good salary. It put a whole cadre of relatively young people in positions of power; suddenly they, rather than the village chiefs, were making the moves and giving the orders that changed the nature of people's lives.

At the beginning, of course, there were not many Micronesians with the desired qualifications, and those available were quickly snapped up. Through the 1960s, as hiring surged more rapidly than the schools could turn out graduates, it seemed that all one needed was a western education to join the new elite. Suddenly what had been limited to the few seemed available to anyone who took the trouble to move through the schools. So it is not surprising that every Micronesian family began to envision great things for its child, and through him, for itself.

That there is a splendid naiveté in this ponzi-like vision

is not germane. It is only indicative of the unreality that afflicts the islands. The assumption that the growth would continue forever, that there always would be jobs for the youngsters who poured half-trained from the new and increasingly inadequate high schools, fixed itself like a delusion on the people—and they are loath to surrender it. But today the growth has stopped and the budgets have leveled out and the employment rolls are falling. Those PICS graduates are still young and are well entrenched in their elite and monied status, and there is no room for newcomers. Naturally the newcomers, imbued as they are with the dreams of unreality, do not respond well to the situation. Thus the linkage between the trouble in Micronesia today and the growth in the 1960s that seemed unending and that shattered all that had gone before.

★ ★ ★ CHAPTER SIX

THE END OF THE DREAM

Despite its real impact, the relative fortune poured into Micronesia has made little physical impression. Today's visitor finds a shock of recognition in the descriptions of ten and twenty years ago, so little has the tattered appearance of the place changed. And now, with the U.S. contribution leveling out and thus diminishing in per-capita terms as the population continues to grow, the chances of physical improvements are fading like the mirage that they probably were.

The United States already has served notice that its contribution will be limited to about $80 million per year—in constant dollars, or with an inflation factor included. Perhaps that decision is a tacit admission that pouring in money did not work; it did not make friends and it did not produce a viable society, and now we propose a holding operation.

Almost from the beginning of the growth period, the Micronesian budget has been squeezed, by grandiose plans and by the ever expanding number of employees whose salaries are geared to American civil-service concepts with automatic raises. As the operating part of the budget has drawn an ever bigger share of the whole, the construction side has shrunk. This means that the growth of the physical infrastructure on which economic development depends—transport, communications, a workable marketing system—has shrunk as well.

This certainly contributes to the fact that the Micronesian economy is almost nonexistent, but the more important point is that the potential of the islands in modern economic terms is pitifully small (see Chapter Eight). And at least partly because the dreams of Micronesia have inhibited real and sensible growth, what little potential exists has hardly been developed at all. Continental Airlines operates a twice-weekly jet service—Air Micronesia—that services district centers and is limited but very useful. Docking facilities have been improved and one is surprised at the size of the ships one sees at Majuro in the Marshalls. But smaller field-trip ships, which frequently break down and lie for weeks awaiting parts, still are the basic transport around the territory. In every other respect the islands have the look of distant outposts, the sort of thing one might expect to find far up the Amazon or in the villages on the distant Arctic rim of Alaska.

The district centers serve as the towns of Micronesia, but the word should be used with caution, for they are nothing like towns in any developed part of the world. They are more rural village than urban center and most of them are crazy collections of little buildings made of concrete or sheet metal or packing cases or thatch strung at odd and individualistic angles, along winding, muddy, pot-holed dirt roads that climb hills and plunge into gullies and twist and turn as if their makers were drinking the fermented juice of the coconut palm as they worked. Here and there old Japanese buildings huddle heavy and secretive with their narrow

windows and their blackened walls. An occasional govern-
ment-building reaches a second story, and one often sees
Quonset huts looking dented and worn but as serviceable
as ever. A few small warehouses stand near the dock areas,
though several districts are still without refrigerated warehousing. Occasionally there is a gasoline pump—which is
often closed. Cars creep slowly through the ruts, growing
old before their time (between shaking on the roads and
rusting in the salt air, two years is their usual life). Here
and there one finds a bit of paving, a mile in Palau, a mile
now broken up in Yap. Saipan, which is severing itself
from Micronesia, is more developed, and Majuro, which is
wealthier than its sister districts, imported paving equipment recently and began spreading asphalt everywhere.
Electricity is supplied entirely by diesel power and is never
to be relied upon, and telephones hardly exist. Yap has one
real restaurant that serves dinner from six to seven: this is
in the one hotel, which has ten rooms. Continental Airlines
has built incongruously modern hotels at Palau, Truk, and
Saipan as part of its franchise deal, but otherwise hotels in
Micronesia are chancy affairs. There used to be laundry service at the biggest hotel in Majuro. But the dryer broke and
since it rains every day it is hard to dry clothes on a line;
and altogether, it seemed better not to have a laundry. In
most centers there is one passable restaurant to which everyone goes, so that meal by meal one sees the same diners
eating the same food. There is little fresh fish and almost no
fresh fruit available in these restaurants because there is no
system for regular procurement. In each district center there
is a handful of stores with mostly empty shelves but unex-
pected oversupplies. Paper towels, napkins, tissues, toilet
rolls in startling profusion; moustache wax and an odd po-
made; beer, mostly Schlitz; shelf after shelf of canned meats
and what might be called the disgrace of Micronesia—
canned tuna, caught in Micronesian waters by Japanese
trawlers, canned in Japan, and returned for sale. Looking at
all this you realize the significance of the merchandising

and distribution systems built up in developed countries. Micronesia has none of the understanding and reliable commitment and masses of capital and lines of credit and capacity for projecting and planning that makes things go. The only things that seem to run well are the bars and the tatterdemalion movie theaters where, at the time of my visit, Kung Fu was in the ascendancy.

And yes, down the rutted road a bit there is a gorgeous beach where the palms stand watch and the trades sweep in from the sea. Rain slashes down and a few minutes later the sun turns the standing water to steam. The air is languid, moist, heavy, sweet with flower scent. This is still the south seas—but you will look in vain for the legends of old; this is the Made-in-U.S.A. version.

Despite the official talks between the United States and Micronesia concerning its future status and despite the rising Micronesian nationalism, it seems certain that the United States will continue to be the dominant force in the islands for the forseeable future. American interests are perceived as overriding, and there really is no chance of their being abandoned, which may be part of the reason that though the talks have dragged on since 1968, a territory-wide solution seems as far away as ever.

Ironically, the rise in Micronesian nationalism coincided with the insertion of massive American funding aimed at drawing Micronesians closer to their patron. And the mechanism for Micronesian separatism grew from the expansion of democratic institutions, which Americans assumed would demonstrate the superiority of their methods.

The government was expanded, and articulate, intelligent, newly educated Micronesians moved into positions of new power. The Congress of Micronesia was formed by U.S. order and this gave Micronesians a central forum. It was assumed that the Congress would serve in tandem with the executive, but this is not how politics works. In retrospect, it was obvious that the Congress would have to stake out separate and ultimately conflicting ground if it was to be a force, and that to fail to do so would be destructive to the local power of its members, almost all of whom owed their selection to power they already had, rather than the opposite.

The effect of this movement of the Congress was to enhance Micronesian unity and the concept of Micronesians as a people whose interests hardly coincided with American interests. Peace Corps agitation added to the idea of an emerging Micronesian self which need not necessarily be subordinate, and each year the schools turned out more youngsters whose vision, at least, had been broadened. The world reaction to Vietnam and the emergence of other underdeveloped nations added momentum. The return of Okinawa to Japan gave Micronesians a keener understanding of the strategic importance of their islands.

In mid-1966 the Congress of Micronesia made the first move that led to the formation of formal negotiating sessions on how the future was to be resolved. These began in 1968 and at this point it probably was too late for the United States to take what earlier it could have had for the asking. When it decided that the Micronesians really were serious, the United States collected itself and offered what had been its intention all along, to make Micronesia its own as a commonwealth or as an unincorporated territory similar to Guam. It was a huge step, which went unnoticed by the American public, because it meant permanently adding territory that was very distant and was peopled by a distinctly foreign culture. Perhaps because it was such a huge step, the United States was dismayed when the Micronesians summarily rejected it.

In what undoubtedly was a National Security Council decision, President Nixon, in 1971, took the talks from the hands of the Department of Interior and appointed Franklin Haydn Williams as his personal representative with the rank of ambassador. (Williams's tour of duty ended in 1976.) Williams heads the Asia Foundation, and old rumors that it had been a CIA conduit fed the militant minority in

Micronesia. Many Micronesians find Williams personally abrasive and he finds them equally irritating. With some justification, he sees them as youngsters play-acting on the world's stage—heady, irresponsible, manipulative. Williams explains readily that the United States wanted much more than it could get in the negotiations and now is just seeking the half-loaf that might remain. That probably is a considerable understatement both of American intentions and of the probable outcome.

The current plan around which both sides are maneuvering calls for Micronesia to have a "free association" with the United States for the next fifteen years. Under this relationship it would handle all of its own domestic affairs and the United States would handle its foreign affairs and its defense matters. The United States would exclude military penetration by other nations and could negotiate for more military bases. And the United States would continue to put some $80 million a year, with adjustments for inflation, into the Micronesian economy. The wrangling has been over the form of this concept—acceptance of which is by no means certain—and the amount of annual support the Micronesians want. Under Williams, the United States has taken a much harder line on how much it will spend, presumably because the earlier largesse proved counter-productive.

Signs abound of the eventual collapse of this concept—to the advantage of the United States. The defection of the Marianas, which the United States encouraged, is the first threat to the overall agreement. The Marianas is the most advanced of the districts and its people seem never to have shared the rising Micronesian nationalism. Guam, which prospers nearby (or appears to prosper; you cannot help but wonder if its plastic prosperity is real), is geographically a part of the Marianas, and Marianas people seem to feel much more related to it than to the nebulous concept of Micronesia. At one point the district tried to annex itself to Guam, which Guamanian voters rejected. As Micronesians turned away from the U.S. relationship, and as the United

States saw its hopes for the islands threatened, the Marianas asked for separate negotiations and the United States agreed. The result was an agreement in principle for the Marianas to become an American commonwealth operating on rather a parallel basis with Guam. Among other things, the United States would get the rights to another big military base on the island of Tinian. Presumably final action on the Marianas cannot come until the whole issue of Micronesia is resolved, but the people of the Marianas held a plebiscite in 1975 in which they approved the commonwealth plan.

The move of the Marianas probably serves the interests and the desires of its people. It also serves American interests, since bases there would bulwark those on Guam, and it probably would not be difficult for the United States to block foreign military adventures in the rest of Micronesia by force if necessary. At the same time, however, it does not seem overly cynical—given the American preoccupation with the military role the islands might play—to assume that the Marianas ploy is part of a larger intention.

Certainly the separation of the Marianas from the rest of Micronesia is destructive to the concept of Micronesia, which always is on the verge of flying apart. As the central and the capital district, it anchored Micronesia. It is disproportionately developed, and its absence will make it harder for the remainder of Micronesia to stand on its own. The Marshall Islands, the next most powerful and developed district, has raised the question of separate talks for itself. If the Marshalls split, Palau might follow. Palau is the next strongest and its people are noted for being more aggressive and more American-like than most Micronesians. The result would be to leave the last three districts, the poorest and most depressed islanders of all, to fend for themselves. Under such circumstances, they presumably would have little choice but to join whatever structure the United States chose to erect. One cannot help but suspect that Ambassador Williams's picture of the United States patiently seeking its half-loaf is disingenuous to a fault.

Thus the story is anything but over. Micronesia and the United States will remain inextricably linked, and as the seeds planted so casually and arrogantly over the last thirty years mature, the United States will share in their fruit. We will hear a great deal more about Micronesia in the future than we have in the past.

CHAPTER SEVEN

SCHOOLS AND UNREALITY

When you tour Micronesia to look at education, you see the dilemma laid out in full. It becomes ever more clear that while the people see education as the avenue to the new success, their understandinging of the interlocking nature of modern western society is so slight that they remain blind to the plain fact that their own society contains so little that is capable of supporting the new ways. Surely it is the cruelest irony that it is education itself which exacerbates their blind hopes, as year by year it trains their children away from the old culture and toward an ambiguous academic form that is supposed to be consistent—in some unknown way—with the modern world and with its advantages.

So, perhaps only because it already is too late to turn back and no other road presents itself, Micronesians press ahead on education. Almost angrily they press elementary students to compete for high-school positions, and they press

American officials and their own political leaders to enlarge high schools so that everyone may go. But still, the government jobs are taken, and the basic society offers new graduates little to do, and the picture steadily darkens. So education stands both as metaphor for the Micronesian dilemma and as a central actor in it. As you visit the educational establishment, notwithstanding the obvious goodwill of those who maintain it, this is the overriding reality that flows through the vignettes of experience.

Yap was a speck on the sea and the 727 came down, and suddenly the island filled the window, dense green, shoalgreen water all around, brilliant beach separating the two like an artist's line of light. The plane buzzed the short runway at two hundred feet to clear it, circled once, and slammed down with gravel flying and the engines screaming in reverse thrust. The fuel truck came out and the ground crew followed. Each man wore a bright red *thu* (pronounced *too*), a cotton sash serving as breechclout with the ends hanging down front and back. They opened the fuel ports in the plane's wings and plugged in the hoses.

There were a hundred-odd people at the thatched station. It was plane day, a twice-weekly event, and people want to see who comes and goes and to pass gossip. Packets of betel nut were for sale in the woven purses in which men who wear *thus* carry their belongings, and Palauans whose island was the next stop hurried off the plane to buy betel nut, for Yap betel nut is widely known as the best in Micronesia. It grows everywhere in thick green clusters that hang from particularly graceful little palm trees.

John Perkins picked me out of the incoming line and Mary Buw dropped a tightly woven hibiscus lei around my neck—a beautiful thing, red as flame—and I was properly welcomed. Perkins, since replaced by a Micronesian, then was the last American district-education director and was one of the most competent Americans I met in Micronesia. He had years of American foreign service in Africa behind him, which gave him more experience with reality than people who served all their time in Micronesia.

The Yap Board of Education met that afternoon in Perkins's office. It rained, as usual, thunderheads boilding up like mountains, the sky blackening. The education office's roof leaked, and Perkins kept an old T-shirt on his desk to mop up the pools of water that formed among his papers. The airconditioner labored and muttered until the damp air took on an unpleasant chill. Presently the board arrived.

The rain stopped, the sky cleared, the sun burst forth. It is time for the meeting. The board has four members: the chairman, Linus Ruamau, who runs a store and hides his growing wealth from the community; Carmen Chigiy, postmistress; Roboman Andrew, a chief of Yap Island; and Bellarmino Hethy of Ulithi, an outer-island chief. A hundred miles of open sea lie between Yap and Ulithi, which is a great curving atoll looking from the air like white stones skipping on the sea. Once, thirty years before, the ship on which I was a seaman drew up at one of those tiny, uninhabited islands, and we trouped ashore for an oddly unsatisfying beer-drinking liberty that ended in a fight. Chigiy (Yapese women do not take their husband's names) is in a postal-service uniform, blue skirt, blue cotton shirt with regulation shoulder patch, and *zoris* (the universal shoe of Micronesia, sandals in the Japanese style now manufactured in rubber). Roboman and Raumau wear shirt and pants. Hethy is dressed in an elaborate *thu*. He is bare chested and has a gold wristwatch. The men wear *zoris* too.

The meeting begins, the members seated around a long government table. It is in English for Perkins's sake. Hethy and Roboman do not speak English, but probably understand it. The other two query the chiefs from time to time and translate for Perkins. Perkins introduces me in the briefest terms and they make polite, noncommittal little noises of welcome. They glide easily, informally, into their meeting and immediately encounter a snag.

The first question is a new orthography of the Yapese language which the board must accept or reject, and the chairman doesn't like it. Neither does anyone else in Yap. It is new and Yapese don't much like new things. Also it is clumsy, irritating, a little ridiculous.

Perkins flings a quick explanatory aside to me, but I already understand the subject. The real issue is bilingual, bicultural education, which is making a comeback in the islands; and the real question around it is more political than educational. Those people who want the islands to remain linked to the United States, which includes the ongoing power structure—and that includes everyone sitting in this room—tend to see the introduction of vernacular training as a device to cut Micronesians away from the English-speaking American fountainhead. In the Marianas this fear is so pervasive that supporting bilingual education is politically dangerous.

The new orthography has been developed by the Pacific and Asian Language Institute at the University of Hawaii under the direction of the same Don Topping who a decade earlier had come out to try to teach the new American teachers something of the overwhelming problems they faced. Topping had sent American linguists to each district to work with a committee of local people to develop acceptable letter forms for each sound. Things had gone predictably. The Americans were on tight schedules, and Micronesians are never on tight schedules. The Americans tended to be positive, and so the Micronesians tended to acquiesce for the sake of form, not conviction. The orthographies generally solved anomalies of pronunciation by adding extra letters and syllables, which made everything look strange and unusual, and since the Micronesians had agreed to nothing anyway, naturally they did not like it. The scene at Yap was being duplicated all over Micronesia.

The chairman says stiffly that he doesn't like the orthography, a surprisingly direct statement. Chigiy nods, agreement unspoken, face somber. The two chiefs look away, taking refuge in the language difference; they will not let it concern them. Chigiy thinks that the old one—a haphazard affair developed by missionaries—is adequate. They mutter over the changes. A text in the old was entitled *Pilung Nu Maday;* in the new it is *Piiluung Nuu Madaay*. They all think the people will react badly. The mission schools teach in English from the beginning and the people like that—after all, the children already speak Yapese. Perkins reminds them that the new bilingual/bicultural training project depends on an orthography and they become cautious, because while they don't like the orthography, they don't want to lose the funds. Perkins guides them toward a solution: They will keep the *i, e, ë, a, u, o, ö* and *ä,* but they will drop *ii, ee, ea, ae, uu, oo, oe, aa,* and they certainly will drop the substitution of *q* for the apostrophes that litter the Yapese language. People are used to those apostrophes. With this decision they will issue a ringing statement, which Perkins will write, reaffirming their faith in the bicultural effort. With this decided, they all feel better. I can see that Topping's troubles are just beginning. Maybe, Chigiy observes, this is the way to make everyone read in English.

Perkins wants to close two schools, both on the island of Yap—Giliman with twenty-eight students and North Fanif with nineteen. The board begins to buck. Chigiy and the chairman frown. The people there won't like it. Perkins says it will be much more efficient and it will help if the board will take a firm stand. At this the chairman becomes quietly but obviously agitated, and Perkins lets the matter slide.

Roboman opens a pack of Winstons and lights one. Perkins's next point is that teachers should not serve as magistrates (which they now do), because they stop school to hold court. Roboman's power now is demonstrated. They confer and Chigiy announces that Roboman will pass a rule forbidding anyone to serve in both roles. The matter is settled. Roboman stubs out the Winston, puts a betel nut in a pepper leaf, sprinkles white lime over it from a small, well-fashioned coconut shell (looking not unlike an old powder horn), folds it neatly, and bites down on it. Hethy seems to have no vices.

When the ships come to the Outer Islands High School at Ulithi with supplies, the students are paid to unload it. Originally they unloaded without charge; it was their food, after all. But education headquarters in Saipan began paying, and now they expect it, two to three thousand dollars a year. Now Saipan, squeezed by ever-tightening budgets, wants the district to assume the cost. The district budget is equally pinched and Perkins thinks there should be no charge.

Chigiy asks if the money goes directly to the students. No, it goes into a scholarship assistance fund for seniors. "I don't know what the people there would think," she says. That is the key question. Hethy lights a Winston; vices after all. Chigiy thinks the decision should be made on Ulithi. Hethy is consulted and gives a fully noncommittal answer. The idea of paying people to do what he thinks they should do for themselves stirs a slow anger in Perkins; the idea of exerting unilateral power stirs an equally deep reluctance in Chigiy. Perkins suggests writing the board of the Outer Islands High School for a reaction. They all like this: it has postponed the question.

Chigiy opens the blue leather purse that is part of her postal-service uniform and takes out a cluster of betel nut. They make a meaty thump when she puts them on the table. She has a supply of pepper leaves and a lime shaker. She folds one together and puts it in her mouth. Hethy adjusts his *thu* and takes a nut and a pepper leaf. His gold watch gleams in the light and I notice the postal-service patch on Chigiy's shoulder.

Another problem: there are three scholarships available and ten applicants. Immediately the question turns, not which three should be chosen but what of the other seven? Nothing is resolved.

There are new complaints, Perkins says, by outer islanders of the Outer Island High School. People say their children come home and do not fit in well. They are disillusioned; perhaps they should stop sending children there. Perkins turns to Hethy. Without awaiting translation, Hethy speaks at length. The reports are correct, this is the feeling. People are dismayed. Children come home to the island with new ideas about the world that have no place there and with a new contempt for the old ways. They are impertinent to their elders and uninterested in coconut lore, and they would like to go off to the district centers. When they do they are likely to get drunk and have trouble.

Chigiy translates all this, nodding in agreement. When Hethy stops she says that now she encounters the same attitude in Yap itself. This effect of education of separating the individual from the community is newly alarming. Perhaps not all children should go to high school. Perhaps parents should be told that school will change their children. Children emerge from school and feel they no longer need listen to their elders. They all shake their heads at this sign of a dissolving society and soon afterwards the meeting ends.

Later, in the post office, Chigiy said that she had heard of people not fitting back in their communities, but she had discounted it. "But now we are seeing people who come home, even from college, and just hang around. And they drink, yes." She saw this not as pressure from the community but as internal pressure within the student; the community is there, it is the student who does not fit in. "Should high schools train for college? Or should we train them to go back to the community and make something of themselves?" She went to PICS and on to Hawaii for two years. "Right now we're trying to do both and we're not very successful at either. We don't think much about it until a subject comes up—should American history be taught in Yap? Every new educator brings a new idea. But, yes, the orientation should be toward staying in the community. And they can, they should—the community does not demand too much."

She was dubious about the language question. "There'll never be a body of literature. Our language is limited. It is a spoken language. We can write letters, but already we have developed so many English words. The very word for Trust Territory—well, the term hardly translates. Our translation means a string of islands or anything that is lined up. It's a wordy language. If you translated something from Yapese to English you would edit it down to a paragraph. Then when you translated it back into Yapese it would have no meaning. Once I translated the Trust Territory code to Yapese; then I couldn't read it without referring back to the original. Perhaps it is better to teach children in English."

The overall problem is how to adapt materials to the many languages of Micronesia. As oral languages they were never written until Protestant missionaries arrived with the idea that every man should read the Bible. Orthographies were compiled haphazardly; no spelling system emerged, nor did a visual sense of words as entities. Language was perceived as combinations of sounds that flowed together to express thoughts. People venturing into the writing of their language still break sounds wherever they please, and often the reader must say the sounds aloud before he can hear the writer's meaning.

The languages are complex but inflexible. There are words for many stages and conditions and varieties of coconuts but few that deal with metal and its forms. Possessive forms are difficult in a society that does not stress possession. The languages often are strained by new concepts, and there are arguments that some of the distress obvious in Micronesia today relates to the difficulty of describing the present. Yet their complexity also makes it difficult to render them in writing. In Chomorroan, words are built from a root by adding prefixes and suffixes—any verb, for instance, is subject to twenty-six affixes, and each makes a different word.

Vernacular education, once the standard in Micronesia, now is making a small comeback in a series of still modest programs that stress true bilingualism. That a child learns best in his own language seems beyond question, though recent United States Supreme Court decisions making bilingual education a constitutional right of minority language students do not apply directly here, since each Micronesian language is the majority language in its district. In Micronesia the argument over the new bilingual approach, once the political question and the usual dislike for change are set aside, turns around the ever-pressing subject of budgets.

I visited the Catholic elementary school at Yap, which has 220 students and charges tuition of $3 a month for the first student from a family, and $1 for every other child. It receives $23 a year per student from the government. When the subject turned to bilingualism the two nuns to whom I spoke fell into a colloquy that was largely between themselves:

Ann: Theoretically, sure it's good to learn to read in your own language, but there's nothing to read in Yapese. My experience is that kids do learn reading and English at the same time. We've got children who take English books out and read them.

JoAnn: I think bilingual would be an improvement—I'd like to see Yapese language integrated into the curriculum.

Ann: Yes, but this isn't a written language. And the kids come expecting to use English.

JoAnn: But in teaching the way we do, we communicate an attitude, that language is just a tool—it seems to discount their culture. Oh, yes, I know the new ways are coming, but I think the people can maintain a balance between the old ways within their culture and the new ways. The question is, what will help them be happy people in their own context? We have no answers. Look at our curriculum—it's totally imported except for social studies.

Ann: Yes, but where are the Yapese books? Where will you get writers? All they have come up with amount to six little books, pamphlets, really.

JoAnn: Well, they should be able to come up with a curriculum.

Ann: But this Yapese reading is nothing. I want them open to reading, and that means English. What do you do in Yapese to open the world to them? There's just one book, the new Bible, [issued by Protestant missionaries, four hundred copies printed in Hong Kong] and it's a best seller, there's a rush on glasses, they've never read a book.

JoAnn: And that's a sign they enjoy it.

Ann: Well, I think education itself should be paramount. I have to think that the cultural movement hurts education because it drains resources.

JoAnn: I think the culture question is the most critical. The question is, how do we make the Yapese student self-fulfilled? I don't know. That's why this is such an important time. We must at least be aware of what we're doing. We always thought proficiency was the answer, and I'm not so sure anymore.

Later, walking me to the gate, Sister Ann said, "I've got to decide soon. And the resources are so short."

The next day, in Perkins's car, we crashed along the incredibly rutted roads to the far side of Yap Island. Everywhere there are ancient stone foundations of houses overgrown with jungle, the basis of belief that at one time sixty thousand people lived on these islands. We passed Linus Ruamau, the board chairman, standing before his store, and he waved.

"Tough to be a businessman here," Perkins said. "If you try to get ahead, the people will pull you back. Going into business demands much consultation. There must be a consensus for it to work. And the businessman must be careful not to seem better than others. Same dress, same house— you know, if he makes money he can't really spend it, so why bother? And the credit issue usually kills him off anyway. He can't refuse credit to the extended family, and the family gets very extended. And none of them understand how credit lines work and the problem of resupply. So when his shelves are empty and his ledger full of credit, he's out of business. Then the suppliers can't collect what he owes them and the whole place gets a bad name."

I mentioned that Chigiy had seemed surprised that graduates didn't fit in. Perkins grunted. "Well, I had a teacher who came back from the University of Guam. He had high hopes, but soon he was drinking heavily and missing class. After five months, he came to me and said, 'John, I have a problem.' And I said, 'Yes.' And he said there was a conflict between his drinking and his teaching. And I asked him what he was going to do about it and he said, 'I've decided to drink.' So I let him go and he wandered around the island for months, wearing nothing but shorts and usually drunk. I saw him the other day and he stopped me and said, 'John, I think I may be ready to come back before long.' And I told him, fine, let me know. He's working his way back in to the community, you see. And another fellow, same thing, he had married a Peace Corps girl. They were both bright, you know, but he began to drink and she worked with him for awhile and then she left; she was upward mobile, American, and he was downward mobile. He's okay now, back in his community."

We came to Gagil School, a small building with wooden walls and a tin roof held in place by hand-adzed beams. Clouds were low and it began to rain. A giant breadfruit tree darkened the yard further. In a first-grade class a small, tough-looking man was teaching math, using sticks tied in bundles with pandanus strands to illustrate sets. He did not use a word of English. The boys wore *thus,* the girls grass skirts. Yap is the only district still using traditional dress. In a third-grade oral English class the teacher, another man, was working hard, the children singing after him in unison. "This is a stick," he shouted, holding a long twig, "this is an end and that—" gesturing "—is an end too." The class, then groups, then individuals repeated the phrase until it took on rhythm, "This is an end and that is an end-too."

This is a table—this is an end and that is an end-too." He
picked up a long ruler. "This shardstick has two ends—this
is an end and that is an end-too." "That shardstick has two
ends—that is an end and that is an end-too." The seventh
grade was reading the *Merrill Linguistic Reader Number 4*,
apparently geared to the second grade, since the story observed that "Dan is six years old." This was one of Yap's
better schools.

We went on to Tamilang School where the sixth grade
was reading English, from *Merrill Reader Number 3*. One
child held his book sideways. "Gus runs his bus. Jim and
Tim get into it . . . the bus gets into a rut . . ." The children read aloud in English but they asked questions in
Yapese and the teacher answered in Yapese. This certainly
was no more than decoding word for word. When I spoke
to the teacher he was barely understandable in English.
Perkins thinks the rote drill is better than this. "The kids
are bright," he said, "and a good teacher can do a lot with
them. But the teachers go too slowly. The whole problem is
that the teacher's background is so limited—ninety-five percent of these kids have never seen a good teacher . . ."

There is something grumpy and frustrated about the educational bureaucracy in Micronesia; it is not satisfied with
itself, nor does it satisfy its clients, but it sees no way to
alter the situation; it is always behind in doing what it is
trying to do, leaving little time and energy for dreaming of
what it might be doing. The fact that its clients are not
Americans and that in culture and heritage they could
hardly be more different than an industrialized, urbanized
people of two hundred million living on a great land mass
is well understood but hardly considered. The consensus is
that this is the course, we are committed; the consensus
also is, perhaps a bit less definitely, that it may be the
wrong course, or at least, not a very useful course.

Taken on its own terms—that of an American model—it
compares poorly. The bulk of its teachers have no more

than a Micronesian high school education, which is not a powerful teaching base, and some have less. It spends less than $330 per student per year; and this figure is heavily distorted in that it includes large expenses not usually a part of education. Jim Hawkins observed in 1969, as he completed a tour as director of education, that it is "an unformed educational system transposed onto a poor model of a typical American system. . . . emphasis is placed on career objectives which frequently have little meaning for Micronesian youth. Even worse, Americans have fostered false education values which now are held by many Micronesians and which may well lead Micronesia into political and economic difficulties."* Dirk Ballendorf believes the situation is getting steadily worse; the population is increasing, the facilities and manpower applied to the situation are shrinking, the gap between promise and performance is widening. The system's students lag up to five years behind students in American systems. Several years ago a test suggested that about two percent of the Trust Territory's high-school seniors would have a reasonable chance for success in an American college. American tests obviously are biased, but I believe these results are accurate.

And yet, it has some positive points once you get beyond the comparison which its form invites. Given the realities, the structural nature it has developed, the limitations imposed on it by funding and terrain, I think there is no contradiction in saying it can be impressive, it tries hard, and it does a lot with its resources. Its people generally are young and enthusiastic and one finishes a tour with a strong sense that educators there care about the schools and the students and the quality of teaching. The children seem interested, disciplined, willing, and, of course, charming, even allowing for the effect of the visitor. The schools operate on Micronesian time, which is to say more or less, but when they are functioning, the teachers are in control and some learning is happening.

* Unpublished manuscript.

Furthermore, I did not meet a single instance of anyone trying to hide anything from me or to make anything appear better than it was. I was welcomed everywhere, taken to schools I asked to see, left free to talk to teachers and children whom I chose, shown all the records I asked to see. I found it impossible to exhaust the patience of these people, and I came away grateful and respecting them as individuals, if not in admiration of their system. And, of course, they are not that admiring of it themselves.

The Department of Education headquarters is in an old auditorium on that former CIA base atop the highest mountain on Saipan, and it seems cut off from the districts. District directors report to and draw their funds from the local district administrator, and since each district has a different language, different cultural attitudes, and different problems, they orient much more to their internal situation than to directives from headquarters. All district directors now are Micronesians, as is David Ramarui, the territory's education director. There is a persistent move throughout the territory to reduce American employees, partly as policy and partly because Micronesians draw less pay. At both the district and the territorial levels, everyone seems to spend an unconscionable amount of time satisfying the paper demands of the bureaucracy. Ramarui agrees that the questions of where education is going are more crucial than ever but adds that he is so immersed in structural and bureaucratic demands that he lacks the resources to address them.

Distance and the cost and difficulty of transportation dominate all considerations in the territory. The system spends about $186 per pupil in elementary schools and almost $600 per pupil in high school. High schools are necessarily boarding schools, and most of their extra costs are for boarding and transporting students. Much of school-building construction funds thus go for dormitories rather than for classrooms.

Education is only theoretically universal through the eighth grade, since there is no way for an administrator to know what goes on in distant island schools. An accepted rule of thumb is that of the normal 180 days of instruction per year, outer-island elementary schools give about 100 days.

Education is the largest segment of the Trust Territory government, with the biggest budget and the most employees. In fiscal year 1975 the Trust Territory government budgeted $12,855,600 for all of education, including unusually expensive administration. HEW enrichment programs spent $2,459,000. There are 228 elementary and 22 secondary schools (including some junior highs), which in 1975 were expected to have 28,200 elementary and 6,000 secondary students. There were 1,402 elementary teachers and 502 high-school teachers, of whom 128 were Americans, almost all employed in high schools. In addition, there are about one hundred Peace Corps volunteers teaching in Micronesia. There also are 15 church-supported, private elementary schools and 13 such high schools, to which the Trust Territory offers modest financial help. In 1974 there were 4,742 children in these schools.

It is graduation day at Airai School on the island of Babelthuap, which adjoins the headquarters island of Koror in the district of Palau. This is a country school, eight grades in eight classrooms that are thirty feet square and built in a single line so that the breeze sweeps each from side to side. The other building—office and cookhouse—was built by the Japanese, and its massive concrete walls are blistered still from strafings now some thirty years past.

A partition opens between the last two classrooms and in the resultant room, sixty feet long, the eighth Commencement Exercises are being held. There is no electricity, but the room is light and airy. It has an eight-foot overhang against the sun on each side and shutters open to the breeze. When it rains the wooden shutters are closed and the room becomes dark and stuffy and makes study difficult, so teachers often do not bother to come on rainy days.

A big, lovingly drawn sign gives the class aim, *Udalsuu-llomes ma klechad,* which translates rather roughly as Thinking/wisdom as a way of life. Klechad is pronounced with a clucking quite different for an American tongue. The room is full of parents holding leis which they will bestow on the new graduates. They have come to the school as to church, bearing baskets of food, each basket freshly woven this very morning of green pandanus fronds and containing a green drinking coconut and baked chicken and breadfruit sticks and arrowroot pudding and carameled tapioca and sliced taro—altogether more things than the eye can absorb or the stomach accept at once. The people are proud, it is the event of the year, and dignitaries are seated in places of honor.

A processional sounds scratchily on a hand-cranked record player and the graduating class marches in, awkward in new black shoes, and all the more self-conscious because they are of a society which usually expects children to be as nearly invisible as possible. But all is different on graduation day; even the twin posts on the playing field outside (which in fact are palm poles which competing relay teams climb), look today like usual goal posts. The graduating class sings the Anthem of Micronesia, which is surprisingly pleasant—"We are a people of oceans. . . . we will work together to make these islands another promised land." The Micronesian anthem, of course, is in English, for having nine languages is like having none. But Dr. Yuzi Mesubed speaks in Palauan and I listen bemused. The school is built on a ridge where the breeze sweeps in from the Philippine Sea and I watch the deep blue water restless and glittering under the sun. Five hundred miles away lies the southern tip of the Philippines. The sun pours down until the moving palm fronds and the banana trees seem nearly black and a flame tree blazes outside. Suddenly from the torrent of

Palauan the phrase leaps out, "No way!—because he has not practiced . . ." and I am reassured that this is a universal graduation speech.

Airai is typical of Micronesian schools. A few in the district centers are much larger, and there are still many smaller schools on outer islands; but most have eight rooms, often in an old and in a new building, built athwart the trades, with a generous playground, a toilet shack built over a pit, and an office-storeroom tucked against the end of a building. They usually have a battered, chipped, mildewed look, with mud splashed about and signs of bare feet and crayons on the walls. Now and again one sees a piece of playground equipment; at a country school in Ponape it was rusted and forlorn as if it excited nothing in the children there. Most buildings are of concrete block with corrugated metal roofs. Ceilings are rare. Rural schools have no electricity but it does not matter—there is always enough light in Micronesia. Some buildings have mesh on the windows, and some have glass louvers, but most have solid shutters attached at the top that stand horizontally from the building when they are open and bang down tightly at night and during typhoons.

The best building I saw was at Saipan, built by the Japanese of heavy timbers and corrugated roofing metal. Its huge overhang shielded the sun's glare and meant the windows rarely had to be closed against rain. The roof was raised with additional venting which seemed to sweep a current of air along its undersides, and it was both the gentlest light and the coolest building I found. The worst was a mainland-U.S. model designed for airconditioning, which was not air conditioned.

In the Marshalls one often sees a bright, almost shiny metal building that rises like an apparition, its panel dented and crumpled but its core as solid as ever. Known universally as Eniwetok buildings, they have come unscathed through nuclear bomb tests and have been dismantled, shipped here, and reassembled.

The virtues of concrete-block buildings with big windows and little adornment become increasingly apparent as you move through the districts. At Saladak School in rural Ponape, for instance, the first of two buildings had been made of block. The second, barely two years old, was of prefabricated plywood, and already it was peeling, blistering, and sagging. It will return to the earth while the concrete building serves on.

A two-story vocational-education building in the Marshall Islands is made of metal, and though it was only a year old when I saw it, rust ran like pus down its sides, and no amount of repainting could save it. Fixtures, braces, downspouts, window framing, seemed to be dissolving before one's eyes. The building cost about $650,000.

Costly construction and constant delays are basic problems in Micronesia. Shipping adds some forty percent to the cost of building materials. Most serious building is done by Koreans or Filipinos, but work often is delayed for months. Shipping is so uncertain and pilferage so serious that some building projects take years. A new high school of seven small, prefabricated buildings at Yap, costing about $700,000, had been four years under construction when I visited and still was not finished.

I know of no elementary schools with libraries, and books are at a premium throughout Micronesian schools. The three thousand-volume library at Yap High School is the only library in the district and serves schools and public alike, though reading is not a major activity in Yap. Elementary teachers keep stacks of tattered books on shelves and hand them out to students. Many are routine texts in English from American publishers, while Micronesian textbooks actually are slender pamphlets of hardly better than mimeograph quality. Perhaps because this is an oral culture, there is no tradition of valuing books and the children are very hard on them.

When Micronesian teachers walk into their classrooms, they have little going for them but their imagination. And given the lack of course materials, the lack of teaching plans, the scarcity of books, the shortage of material for their own study, and their lack of training, you have to admire them. I saw few patently poor teachers and many who appeared to be engaged and in control.

Of course, first you have to catch them in the act. When I arrived at the Saladak School a half hour after its starting time, three of eight teachers had arrived, and some fifty youngsters were milling about. Classes had not started when I left. Teacher absenteeism is chronic for the same lack of attention to schedules that pervades all of Micronesia.

Training is the key problem for all Micronesian teachers, about two thirds of whom are men. They rely too heavily on rote teaching, because they do not know what else to do, and because most of the materials are in English. Despite a decade of insistence by the school system, neither teacher nor pupil is comfortable in the language. This also makes difficult the introduction of new and increasingly sophisticated curricula. Most teachers I met were not high-school graduates but had a bit of extra training in the various teacher-training programs the districts maintain.

Theoretically the territory's basic teacher-training institution is the two-year Community College of Micronesia, which occupies a Ponape campus that looks like a standard elementary-school site. Apparently the school is not much more effective than it looks. Its graduates emerge only marginally beyond high-school graduates and enter the ranks of the jobless. At one point in 1974, with most of its faculty fired or resigned, it seemed ready to close, a move that hardly could be improved on. Then it reversed itself, rephrased its mission in higher-flown language, and, at last report, the U.S. Congress had taken the first steps to give it a special grant to erect a big, new building. Thus the Micronesian unreality meanders forward.

Curriculum seems to develop by hit and miss. Most curriculum specialists really are teacher trainers, more interested in working with what is than developing something new, which perpetuates the existing system while precluding much thought about alternatives. A certain amount of seeming lip service is paid the idea of materials and training in the context of the Micronesian environment, and so there are readers picturing brown-skinned youngsters and referring to islands and lagoons instead of farms and supermarkets; but in the main the elementary courses remain mostly similar to a standard metropolitan American model with emphasis on academics. Generally, high-school courses are mere expansions of that trend.

From time to time new curriculum schemes flash through the territory, with new materials and specialists from Honolulu flying out to promote them. My impression is that except in the area of language, things nevertheless tend to go along more or less as before. There is the problem of explaining new materials and approaches in so many languages, the constant shortage of materials, and most of all, the fact that subjects like modern math demand sophistication beyond most Micronesian teachers.

The mathematics curriculum dips slightly into the new math, but all that I saw being taught was simple arithmetic. The science curriculum grows out of the Science Curriculum Improvement Study at Berkeley. Al Carr, professor of education at the University of Hawaii serves as a special consultant to Micronesia and tours the districts, helping science-curriculum people master the techniques. He feels the program is ideal where there is a language barrier because it is manipulative and materials-oriented and engages the children in activity. Theoretically the program relies on native materials, but in Micronesia it proved too expensive to collect them and now materials are ordered from the United States. When I saw Carr at Majuro he was demonstrating the study of pressure with a syringe that popped a cork when the plunger was pressed. The program's chief problem is that teachers tend to lose the expensive materials, which says a good deal about its reception. The pro-

gram does not generate much enthusiasm; something
stressing marine biology and tropical botany would be
more useful.

The idea of a Micronesian-oriented social-studies program is spreading swiftly because it is in tune with the rising sense of Micronesian nationalism. For years Micronesian children were taught standard American civics and
even American history. "My God," said a Micronesian poli-
tician, "why should I grow up knowing about George
Washington and knowing nothing about my own islands?
But I did." Now some high schools teach a Pacific-peoples
course which deals with American history when it describes the concept of democracy. Some schools also bring
in community people—storytellers, net makers, naviga-
tors—who can help children understand their own culture.

The issue is complicated by the number of languages and
by Micronesia's lack of a clear identity. Local-language publishing is difficult. The schools at Yap have developed pamphlets for the first couple of grades but after that must rely
haphazardly on various texts. There are a number of fitful
projects to collect myths and folklore on tape and to tran-
scribe them, either in the vernacular or in English. In the
Marshalls, Emi Mukaida is developing a program of
legends, stories, and any other reading matter she can find.
She wants to develop thinking, to help children understand
other cultures and thus better understand their own, and to
expand social skills. Considering the language problems
most teachers have, she seems quite optimistic.

The Marianas are the most advanced district. A prolific,
dedicated woman named Frances Baker has developed there
the best social studies program in Micronesia. Its draw-
backs are that it is all in English and the writing is not of
high quality. But Mrs. Baker, writing it all herself, has
emerged with seven big, well-illustrated books dealing, in
order, with the family, the village, the island, the Mariana
Islands, Micronesia, the islands of the Pacific, (which was
difficult, she said, because it was necessary to place Micron-

esia at the center of the world, where it is not often perceived) and the Pacific Coastline—Alaska, British Columbia, California, Mexico, Panama, Australia, China, Japan.
In the high-school program, she relies on two books on
Micronesia written by Father Hezel at Truk, and on a couple
of American texts she considers almost useless.

Hezel's two books are considered quite sound and among
the most sensitive writings on Micronesia, which also
speaks to the educational level there. Hezel has rethought
the matter and now believes there is some cultural arrogance in his writing books on Micronesia for Micronesians.
He probably will not do another.

As you tour through the islands, you find the people
there are so unaware of the nature of life in the modern
world and of how societies and economies interlock in the
world community that you begin to wonder if the world
you know is still out there. It really seems that one function
of education might be to provide enlightenment that could
penetrate the ignorance—the oblivious unawareness—that
buffers Micronesia from reality. Gradually I formulated a
little statement that outlined the unreality factors, and most
knowledgeable people agreed with its thrust. Then, I asked,
couldn't there be some sort of reality training in the schools,
something that would connect Micronesia with the way the
world is? It was not a popular question.

At the Marshall Islands High School in Majuro, however,
I found the principal, Bill Nelson, teaching a course that
seemed close enough to my ideas to force me to rethink
them. Watching him slog uphill with his students in a class
on "contemporary problems" was one of the more discouraging things I saw in Micronesia. The class textbook is
an airmail edition of *Newsweek*, and the classwork is to
discuss the issue. Though some forty seniors take the class,
it was the end of school when I visited and only three girls
and a boy were there. Nelson said the class was slow going
because he had to explain so much: "How do you explain
the term 'cliffhanger' when the highest summit in the Mar-

shalls is thirty-three feet?" But he believes the students learn. Could it be given to the whole school? Well, only with adequate faculty, which means an expatriate with an inquiring mind who cares a lot. And could it expand to the community? Only expatriates would come, he thought.

Nelson is a small, somewhat peppery man with reddish-hair, near fifty, and a rather gifted teacher, able to quick-shift about the world with imagination. When I came in, he was talking about Patricia Hearst, it being the period immediately after her apparent conversion to her captors' views:

He forces the class to distinguish the concepts of guilt and innocence and the presumption of innocence. He points out the magazine's care to avoid slander and goes on to discuss slander. How could Patty have changed so quickly? Had she really changed? They think so, so at least they have read the story, but the going is very slow. He can hardly get them to speak. He draws exaggerated pictures which amuse them, but not enough to get them to participate (obviously my presence was inhibiting, but I think that was not a primary factor). Nelson talks about how easy it would be to disappear, to change one's name, to get a new social security number, how one would do it, and in the process he gives implications of the nature of society in the United States, its magnitude and range and mobility and the land mass on which it lives.

He moves to what she would do if she went to Mexico, and then to what Mexicans are like—they are like Marshallese. The idea intrigues: Mexicans like Marshallese. This is the first time they have heard such a thought. He pushes them for abstractions: What do you think of Patty? They don't know.

What does the magazine cover mean—Indira Gandhi and a mushroom cloud. Who is she? Who was the other Gandhi? Quickly he explains the British role in India, the economic aspects of colonialism, the political and military control of the British, then moves into non-violence as a revolutionary concept. He talks about peaceful resistance, about India's problems on the borders of Nepal, about the dismemberment of India, the Pakistan problem, and before he brings this back to the Symbionese Liberation Army, I see that he is giving them a feel for the world's shape, its geography, its immensity, and the immensity of its peoples, all with problems and cultures and attitudes that are foreign to the Marshall Islands. They listen, attentive but leaden.

There was a certain gallantry to this teaching, a tour de force, one man's stand against the black blight of creeping non-knowledge—but oh, how it revealed the immensity of the task ahead!

Vocational education is something that the people apparently need and equally apparently do not want. Their attitude toward it reflects their attitude toward work and thus relates to the overall dilemma that grips them. If they ever are to be self-sufficient, the achievement will turn around work. Presumably at some point the relationship between work and possessions and even survival in a money economy will become more clear and then it will be useful to know laboring skills. In the meantime there is a shortage of fresh vegetables and fresh fish in the district centers; canned fish is a large import item; automobiles collapse in two years; and building is done by skilled workmen from Korea and the Philippines who hire Micronesians to labor as hod carriers because they do not know how to do more and are not reliable in their work habits.

So vocational education could be valuable, though it probably cannot be successful until the people want it. In the meantime—because they do not want it—the education department is reluctant to make it a required course, though some districts do so. There is wide agreement that there should be vocational education in elementary school, but in fact it is offered only in high school except for elementary-school gardens.

The territory's commitment to vocational education is

serious enough, but it does not seem to get much for its money. The real work needs are in mechanical repair, construction, commercial agriculture, and some form of commercial fishing, though it would not necessarily have to be competitive with the world's fishing fleets that ply Micronesian waters. It would be a great help simply to supply a local fish market. In Saipan, however, when an American vocational-education specialist announced a class in lagoon fishing, he was dismayed when only five of seven hundred students applied. The Micronesian position was that they already knew how to fish, why go to school for that?

Traveling through the districts, one sees some developments. The garden at Airai School produces enough vegetables to feed the children at noon, and it is experimenting with flowers to be sold for making leis. The Palau High School has always emphasized vocational education—harking back, perhaps, to that Japanese carpentry school. Now it wants all its students to take a variety of vocational subjects in the first two years, to stream into a particular subject, and to become proficient in the second two years. Both parents and academic teachers (who fear they will be displaced) are resisting, and the students seem to feel that little has changed. The school already has an elaborate vocational component, however, including a group that built several small houses. Alfonso Oiterong, the director of education at Palau, has started a school fair for agriculture products and handicrafts, thus encouraging social studies and vocational education at once. The fairs are so successful that now kids tend to drop all other school work two months before the fair begins. At Yap High School, a gifted Micronesian mechanics instructor keeps an old truck running long past its normal lifespan, but seems to impart relatively little of this knowledge to his students. When I passed through they were industriously grinding an old file into what looked to me like a first class fighting knife, though I was assured later that that hardly could be the case.

Ponape is the closest thing Micronesia has to a potentially

rich agricultural area, and its agriculture program is the strongest I saw. It is a four-year course that starts with the cultural meaning and some of the science of plants, moves in the next to animal husbandry and vegetable planting, goes in the third to the study of plants, soil, nutrition, and so forth, from a commercial viewpoint, and in the last year moves into farm machines and marketing. I was intrigued by the implications of the fact that in the month before I arrived, 77 bell-pepper plants in the garden produced 110 pounds of peppers which sold in the district center for fifty cents per pound. That established a market's existence, but even more, I thought, it established the unreality of a system that could not respond to that need beyond 77 pepper plants in the school garden. Another interesting point is that when you talk to the agriculture students there, it turns out they do not expect to go into farming—they expect to become teachers of agriculture and work for the government.

The territory's largest effort in vocational training is the Micronesian Occupational Center at Palau, with a budget approaching one million dollars. MOC takes high-school graduates and is considered a place of higher learning. Having been conditioned to seeing diligence, an interest in excellence despite limited means, and a sensitivity to culture in the schools, I was disappointed and finally disgusted by MOC. A great deal of money was spent here in the late 1960s to build large new buildings and to fill them with expensive equipment. It was built for 500 students but had only 250 when I visited. Its instructors in the main are not trained in vocational education but simply are skilled in trades. The secretarial instructor had been a secretary who tired of her work. Another instructor had been a mechanic in Vietnam. He had all the earmarks of a longtime alcoholic and told me he settled a problem in his class by whipping the student in a fistfight. What would he have done if he'd lost, I asked, and he said, "Guess I'd have caught the next plane out." The dean of students, a former minister, listened approvingly. There is an appallingly colonial air here—the sense of an American enclave dropped intact, so that you look around for the PX. The dean of students carried a stick which he poked and slashed at students in what he conceived to be a friendly way, but I noticed how many responded with a moment of rage that was quickly covered with a smile.

I saw many shops in Micronesia, and my impression of the MOC shops was that little was happening there. It was a quiet time and many students were away, but there was no sign of anything going on, of real projects, of long term engagement, and since most students are there for two years, there should have been. Yet there was a fatness to it—every high school in Micronesia has a little sewing room where girls struggle to make clothes, and it was revealing to see that in the MOC sewing room, with modern machines and elaborate equipment, the dresses looked no different than those the high-school girls made. The only thing I saw that looked genuinely useful was a production line for making concrete block; at least it made a lot of block. Complaints from all over the territory say that MOC graduates are too little trained to do skilled work but feel they are too well trained to stoop to unskilled work. It was a sad and discouraging place.

Micronesian teachers are academically weak, but they are weakest of all in their ability to speak and certainly to teach English. At Laura School, thirty miles from the district center at Majuro in the Marshalls, and at the very opposite end of the atoll, I met Anko Billy, who was acting as the school's principal. He was an engaging man with a warm smile who was almost incapable in English, though he teaches oral English. Our conversation lurched hopelessly as he smiled and murmured and stared out the window, waiting for me to go away. I slowed and simplified my words, but I never found his level. There is a new road from Majuro to Laura and I asked him if the road had changed things. Eventually he perceived my meaning and found a vent for his frustration: he got angry, indicating that questions about roads were for engineers, not educators.

Most teaching in Micronesia is in the vernacular because few teachers are proficient in English. Since most materials are in English, the whole learning process is severed from its intellectual source (whether American books should be the intellectual source is a different question, and one that goes to the heart of the Micronesian dilemma). A few small bilingual programs are being started. The task seems so huge, given the resources, that some educators, like Sister Ann at Yap, are dubious about diverting money from teaching English skills to teaching in both languages. But how educational money can best be spent is beyond calculating now, since that depends on what education's purpose is to be—which depends on what Micronesia is to be—which is a question no one seems willing to address. But the bilingual approach is exciting and obviously would be an improvement. For that matter, any change probably would be an improvement.

Bilingualism was taking two forms, both starting, when I was there. One for the earliest grades began in a single class on Rota Island in the Marianas. It developed material for three grades but lacked the resources to go further and was forced to rely on church books and on an occasional weekly newspaper in Chamorroan to continue vernacular reading. This is the basic problem. The second program aims at grades six to eight and depends on gathering indigenous materials in the vernacular and processing them into a social studies curriculum that combines the student's heritage and language. The potential in this project seems huge.

But as it matures, it too will face the problem of publishing in the indigenous language. The new orthographies are an important early step in moving from oral to written forms and developing terms for new concepts and artifacts. But even when they are perfected, there is still the question of how much material really can be published for the four thousand people on the face of the earth who speak Yapese. The recently published Bible was a smashing best seller at some four hundred copies. Nowhere in Micronesia is there a child's book in a native language that was not developed for school work.

Publishing in under-developed countries is an important question. "One reason backward countries are backward," as Mary Helen Mahar of the Office of Education in Washington put it, "is because they lack information and reading material in their own language." Topping believes vernacular publishing is a real Pacific need, but he also thinks there may be a thousand languages in the area. There may be a thousand on New Guinea alone. It is one thing to transfer an oral language to writing when a million people use it—and quite another when only four thousand use it. It is difficult to imagine a time when the knowledge of the world or a body of indigenous literature will be available in the languages of Micronesia.

This suggests that whatever Micronesia's future, English will be important. Unless it is to split into its parts, it needs a universal language. No lingua franca has developed, and the Pidgin English of the South Pacific would appear as more foreign than English. And at least some of the people need access to a world language as an access to the world itself. Micronesian nationalists, far from perceiving English as a threat, now see the period when the schools taught little or no English as an imperialistic device to sever them from the world.

Nevertheless, except for the educated elite at the very top, few people in Micronesia have more than a faint acquaintance with English. Competence is unusual. As you move through the islands you find that English draws blank stares and mumbles even from recent high school graduates. Their teachers, as it turns out, usually are not much better. Most people have little day-to-day need for or opportunity to use English. Only a few deal regularly with Americans. There is no press in Micronesia, and radio is quite inadequate.

If English is important, therefore, it must be taught. During the 1960s the idea was to have all instruction in English, but by the end of the period it was clear that that was not working. So the schools turned to Teaching English as a Second Language. The system adopted a syllabus developed by Gloria Tate for the South Pacific Commission, which published the material. It was essentially an oral-aural concept that did not begin with reading. Instead, the teacher spoke the words and the children repeated them. Gradually they were led into responses that changed tense or person. The idea was for them to master the patterns of the language orally before they were exposed to the written word and to the problems of decoding, so reading did not begin until the third grade (which is still the case in most Micronesian schools).

Micronesians are oral and group-oriented people, and the children seem to enjoy the rhythmic recitations. I remember a big, no-nonsense woman at Laura School: " 'Ow many bot-tuls 'ave I?" And the children shouting in unison, "you 'ave two bot-tuls!" She took them through a series of bottles, erasers, pencils, sticks, and so forth, which she pulled in rapid order from a big basket. They never seemed to tire, though I thought it a bit mindless. I may have been seeing a well rehearsed routine kept ready for visitors, a common practice in Micronesian schools. There was no way to know. When I spoke to the teacher later, her English was limited.

The children mirror the accents of their teachers, which is a bit like taking a photograph of a photograph: the image gets less sharp with each transferral. The TESL program was designed to be used by teachers who are English-language natives, and it is widely accepted that as the quality of the teacher's language drops, the whole program drops; with the return to all Micronesian elementary teachers, the effectiveness of TESL may be finished.

Reading begins in the third grade with pamphletlike Dick-and-Jane books in English that are illustrated with brown-skinned children and refer to the island and to the reef. One way to view this is that it starts the child two years behind. A curriculum specialist in the Marshalls noted, however, that the program has not gone on Ms. Tate's schedule. The fifteen books in the series were to be finished by the sixth grade, and in fact many students are still working on them in the eighth. At the Marshall Islands High School Bill Nelson estimated that students enter high school with third grade reading and English skills and emerge reading at about the sixth grade level.

Even these reading levels are deceptive since the capacity to read and to deal in the language are not the same. Petrus Tun, now a sophisticated man who is fluent—if not entirely easy—in English, remembered his experiences in learning it. "In my school at Yap," he said, "every day we said the pledge of allegiance and the multiplication tables and other rote English. I knew nothing of what all this meant, but it took only a week to learn and it pleased the teacher. And it wasn't until I went to PICS that I began to get a real grasp of what this was all about, the full meaning of the language. And it was not until I went to the University of Hawaii and took German that I understood the grammar of English. And at this point, my understanding of the structure and the use and flexibility of Yapese became more clear."

The Catholic elementary schools in Micronesia all start English speaking and reading in the first grade. In the Catholic elementary at Palau, which is run by David Ramarui's sister, Martha (they are a remarkable family), general instruction begins in Palauan and changes gradually to English. Sister Martha thinks that by the fourth grade the children are adequate in English. She is grateful for the South Pacific Commission books, which at least use island terms, but she added that as soon as her children are adequate readers they plunge into the Nancy Drew and Hardy Boys series, fascinated by the mystery element. It was like returning to childhood to hear that. Sister Esther Donovan, acting principal at Assumption Elementary School at Majuro, said she starts children in the first grade on both an oral, phonics-oriented approach and on a reading book and thinks that by the fourth grade they are adequate in English. The basic difference in the Catholic schools is their teachers. Most are professionals, many are nuns, and many are expatriates. They are fluent in English and they work (and live) under close supervision, a condition not possible in pubic schools.

Micronesian children are shy and taken aback by direct questions, but my impression of those I saw was uniformly high. They seem to like school—though attendance is erratic, often poor, and may average on any given day two thirds of those enrolled. They accept rote training readily and seem more comfortable in it, shouting answers happily in unison but most are hesitant if asked to answer individually. I saw a number of classes taking tests; individual students did well until they realized I was behind them. Then wrong answers fell so quickly that I had to move away lest I destroy academic careers aborning. I also saw a surprising artistry in many students, especially in drawings, and I never tired of hearing Micronesian children sing.

I found one truly successful school in Micronesia. It is called the Ponape Agriculture and Trade School and is run by a Jesuit priest. It lies some thirty miles up the lagoon and I went in a Boston Whaler with a group of Ponape schoolmen. Here the reef is not made of the great coral heads that blossom from the bottom as in the South Pacific. Instead it acts as a barrier island, slightly underwater except at the lowest tide, with surf crashing against its outer edge. The lagoon it protects inside is as much as a mile wide. Often it is shallow, and people with spears stalk fish that are clear against the sandy bottom. As the water shallowed under the boat I saw sea cucumbers and brilliant blue starfish littering the floor. Fish of a foot or two poked among the luxuriant sea grass. Schools of bright blue fish, each about a half-inch long turned this way and that, like marching troops. A four-foot manta ray drifted lazily away from us, then in sudden alarm surged thirty or forty feet with the same burst of speed I saw in barracuda years ago in the New Hebrides, disappearing and reappearing, so swift and sudden the movement. White terns flew in tandem and argued with each other so sharply that both seemed to have the advantage.

As one runs up the lagoon, the great slopes of Ponape tower to the right, climbing into the clouds, marked with feathery waterfalls that burst down from the rainfall above. The forests march down to the sea and merge with swamps of mangrove, salt-water trees that will rust a nail driven into them. Ponapeans favor homes scattered along the lagoon instead of tight communities, and all along the shore there were houses and churches and here and there a causeway-like dock of stone built out into the water. People in small, outrigger canoes paddled out to the reef to fish. The clouds darkened and lowered, and just as we swept into the bay, which the school overlooks, it began to rain.

The school is the dream and creation of Father Hugh Costigan. Now in his early sixties, Costigan is a Jesuit from New York who once was chaplain of New York City's fire department and remains an honorary chaplain of its police department, which stages a fund-raising rally every year for this school on the other side of the world. Costigan greeted his visitors warmly, but he had better sense than to accompany us on a tour of the school in the rain.

We went to the parish church, a simple wooden building built in 1936 with artfully carved pillars and polished floors on which the people worship. During the war a P-39 pilot came over a rise and gave the building a burst of machine-gun fire before he saw it was a church (or so he said later). He wrote Costigan eventually, sent maps of his bombing run, apologized, and a few years ago came out to spend a week. The islands draw all sorts of people.

Costigan and his boys built all the rest of the school, including a large two-story central building, some thirty buildings in all, including dormitories, classrooms, and shops. They are of concrete block made in the shops of coral sand, which leaches salt and blisters paint; but Costigan insists on repainting so that all the buildings are bright yellow and have an amazing look of competence and cleanliness. Some two hundred boys go to school here from all over Micronesia, and while there is an academic component, the thrust of the school is vocational in mechanics, construction, and agriculture. There are big shops for each, with classrooms attached and a drafting room linked to the construction and woodworking building. The mechanics building is filled with agricultural machines and equipment and a neat row of Yanmar Diesels (which the Japanese manufacturer donated) on blocks. Each year Yanmar takes some PATS graduates for additional training. On a hill overlooking the rest of the school is a garden filled with vegetables; a piggery in which blooded stock is raised; a henhouse full of chickens where eggs are gathered daily. The farm supplies the school, of course, but some produce is left over for sale in the local cooperatives, which, by no coincidence, Father Costigan also organized.

He came to the Philippines before World War II, to Ponape in 1947, and to this distant location as parish priest in 1954. He calls himself a reactionary and he is a radical; he wants people to control their own lives and he believes government should encourage them to do so. When he found the government importing Filipino laborers to build schools and houses, he demanded to know why weren't Ponapeans trained for the work? Because we're in a hurry, the officials said. Costigan has a feel for the ways of the world; he organized a construction co-op and underbid the firms that the government had brought in, and though officials disapproved, there was no way around the man. He enrolled two hundred and fifty people, brought in a master electrician, a plumber, and a supervisor from the Philippines to guide them, and built twenty-seven schools with ninety-nine classrooms, and thirteen teacher's homes. Some of those Ponapeans are still at work in construction.

So: give them some training, some guidance, and a co-op structure (which is more developed today in Micronesia than any other business form and approximates to some extent old communal forms within a democratic, free-enterprise structure) and they could accomplish things. Why not build a school that would put such instruction on a systematic basis? Forty-eight students applied that first year, and he enrolled thirty-six. Nine hundred took the competitive exams in 1974 for fifty entering places. The school opened in 1965, has been building ever since, and now has more or less completed its plant. It functions as a high school, and a few of its graduates go to college, usually for engineering. But most stay in the community and do the work they have learned at the school. Its reputation has spread all over Micronesia, its graduates are sought after for jobs, and it is seen as equal in desirability with Xavier, the purely academic Catholic high school.

Costigan finds that mechanical and construction graduates are well employed but agricultural graduates have more trouble. He is trying to develop small farms in the community and a co-op that can handle marketing and can purchase the equipment for membership use that no small farmer can afford.

It is a remarkable place—but how do you institutionalize a remarkable place? Costigan spends about $1,300 per student each year. He spends part of each year fund-raising, traveling all over the world, and arriving in New York in late October for the New York Police Department dinner. Hanging from a peg in his office is a blue windbreaker, with an NYPD emblem on it and a gold badge. He will not use all the money he collects—he is trying desperately in the time left him to build an endowment. He wants $1 million—and has about half of it in pledges and in actual gifts. He is an old Irish priest, half piety and half blarney, and he talks of his school as of a vision. We talked two hours and in the midst of it he looked up and saw a Ponapean at the door. He shifted suddenly to Ponapean and settled what the man wanted and then turned to me. "I have a rule that I never keep a Micronesian waiting while I talk to an American. They know that if I do, it only is for the most important reason. I'm their guest, you see, as well as their priest."

The shops are clean and bright, the agriculture area thriving, the buildings freshly painted. The students finish here and go on to what Costigan insists are active, functioning lives, working with tools and the soil and in their own cultural environment. They go on to Japan and to the United States for training—which they survive—and they return still functioning people, without the dislocation found nearly everywhere else in Micronesia. The faculty is strong and dedicated, some priests, some Americans, some PATS graduates turned into teachers. Altogether, even discounting a bit for Father Costigan's enthusiasm, it seems successful both in its operations and in the lives its graduates are making for themselves. Even at $1,300 a year, which public schools cannot spend, it is a bargain. Indeed, it is a microcosm of excellence set in a sea of mediocrity.

And given all that, and the priest's enthusiasm and the strands of his life that are worked into the block of the buildings, you almost hate to ask if it is transferrable, if it can be institutionalized. Does it take a Costigan to make it go? Shadows fell across the man's sunny face for the first time. No, he said, a little stiffly, almost coldly, certainly not; I am not the indispensable man; and other schools like this can be started, should be, and I'm sure will be. I hope he is right, for I didn't see much else in Micronesian schools that worked.

★ ★ CHAPTER EIGHT
★

THE DILEMMA

The mounting frustration that I found so oppressive in Micronesia turns, in part, around the schools. The people thrust in their children, and the schools turn out graduates as if a working society awaited them. But it does not, and so everything begins to break down. You see this very clearly at Truk, which is the most crowded district and the most troubled. The pot-holed dirt streets are filled with people, and drunks appear even by day, sodden and staggering in the hot coral dust. The man who swung his machete at Francis Hezel seemed symbolic of the trouble there; quietly the word is passed to visiting Americans that it would be as well if they were not abroad at night.

Here people press against the public high school as if it were the liberty gate. It is large for a Micronesian school and it is growing rapidly. It stands on a hill in buildings of surprisingly atypical modern architecture. The principal, Robert Kaufman, had kept his office in an older building farther up the hill. It had wooden louvers which Kaufman set against the sun so that the light was cool and soft. The breeze swept up from the sea and washed the building from side to side and you wanted to stay there and talk and not go back out into the heat and the anger of the place. Kaufman spoke slowly, almost phlegmatically, answering questions and explaining facts without judgments and without once admitting by tone or expression the implications of what he said.

The school had grown so rapidly that now it consisted only of the eleventh and twelfth grades, being fed by five junior high schools. The screening process is between elementary and junior high school, which takes about two thirds of all elementary students. They pour from junior high to high school in ever greater numbers.

"This is our first year as a two-year school," Kaufman said. "Last year, with three grades, we had about five hundred and fifty. This year—with just two grades now—we have five hundred. We'll have eight hundred next year, a thouand the next, twelve hundred in the year following that. These are solid projections. We've alrady approved bids for the buildings we'll need."

I had talked that morning with Truk's employment counselor, a frustrated man who spends his days in search of jobs that do not exist. And I asked Kaufman, did he suppose these graduates streaming from his school would find work?

"No," he said, "no, I don't think so. There's not much for them to do. It's not that they lack skills—we've got many kids with skills. We've got good typists coming out of school, for example. Maybe one out of thirty will be hired, maybe two. But they all could do the work if there were jobs.

"It's just that education is years ahead of economic development. There is no clear idea of how economic development will grow, though the schools could educate for whatever was needed. We'll have two hundred and thirty graduate this year and perhaps a hundred go on to college. They jump at a chance to go but they all come back. Twenty-seven graduates of the University of Guam came home this year, and more from Hawaii and the mainland, and the hundred going will come back. And, well, the situation may get ugly.

"I think the drinking problem—and believe me, it's real—is out of frustration. We have some four hundred and fifty boarding students and there is no way to keep them occupied during the evenings and weekends. We have house parents staying with them, but they're not very effective with some fifty kids apiece. Next year we'll have more students but fewer house parents because our budget has been cut again.

"I really don't see what fundamental changes we can make until there is a direction for us to go. All we can do is upgrade what we have, and of course, there's lots of room for that. We can upgrade English and improve the shops and—"

And will that change anything? I asked.

"Not really," Kaufman said. "There still won't be any jobs."

Chutomu Nimwes is the district director of education at Truk. He is a former member of the Congress of Micronesia, a big, physically powerful man with a quick mind and an excellent command of colloquial English. He too thinks about the problems Kaufman sees, though from a larger perspective, and like Kaufman he too talked steadily, as if the questions really ran behind thoughts that are before him constantly.

"People send us their children to be equipped for jobs, any jobs. They come to the government begging for jobs for their children who have just completed high school. They come to my office and sit where you're sitting and cry. Now we turn out more and more high-school graduates, but there are no jobs.

"What we need are goals. What do we want? Why are we

educating our people? To do what? We know there are no jobs. For a time vocational education was the big answer, so we built the Micronesian Occupation Center [at Palau]. The economy could absorb the first class, but then came the second class and the majority were jobless. They couldn't stand on their own—there is no capital to start cottage industries even if they knew how. So today, you see, I am pessimistic about education, either academic or vocational.

"We send them away to college and this year many will come back and I am not sure they will find work. And more will come next year. Unemployment is our problem—we are loaded with graduates without jobs. And I have no answers.

"In the past, when communal living was strong, everyone helped everyone else as a matter of course. It is the way things were. Now it is not that easy. Now, in the markets, you see them selling food, food that always before was a gift, made to relatives and friends. But it would be very difficult today for someone to expect that the next one would help him out. Even among brothers and sisters, they sell things, they expect payment. So, to stay as we are will be difficult, but to go back, well, that also would be difficult.

"The old subsistence economy depended on a communal approach. It is a different matter entirely to do it individually. I don't think we can turn back to old ways. We have been jerked into today and we must stay."

Well, I asked, couldn't education at least be brought in line with the very realities he was describing?

"That would be very tough," he said. "I went out and solicited reaction to the idea of making education consistent with the economy and I got a very negative reaction. When we selected high-school students on the basis of scores, parents, legislators, even the Congress of Micronesia attacked me. Oh, the argument for being sensible was not well received.

"I think this problem is about ten years old. I began to be aware of it in the late 1960s. That is when I resigned from the Congress of Micronesia and came back to education. But even if the acceleration hadn't come, the status quo couldn't have held. The population explosion would have shattered it. I think the break from the communal came at that time and it can't be rescued.

"Oh, of course, the unreality issue goes far beyond just the disparity of the budget—but it is coming to a head now over unemployment. Education and the economy should go together. One should wait for the other; we should have delayed education. But people have learned to expect a lot. Education has opened their eyes. Not long ago about a hundred students walked through the education depart-ment carrying signs that said, 'We have no jobs.' They didn't say anything, but you must understand that in Mi-cronesia, that is a most radical act, it has never been done and people were very shocked.

"I think there will be many more such acts. I am sure that there are many social problems coming. There will be much mistreating of people and times will be bad. And then peo-ple may be used like carabaos."

Yet people want the schools, as harried American educa-tors keep insisting. Those graduates walking through Nim-wes's office with their signs are not seeking a new ap-proach; they want what seems to have been promised. When Nimwes tries to introduce a little common sense into the equation, his people denounce him. They are not ready for any hard lessons in reality.

Since the early 1960s, almost as if American educators suspected there was something dirty in what they were doing, their annual reports have insisted that they were responding to the demands of the people. Was more required of them than blind response to those blind de-sires? It would seem so, since it was their equation that produced the desires.

The question does not fall, of course, between educating the Micronesians or sending them back to their islands to

pick coconuts. Those are false alternatives. Obviously Micronesians are going to come into the world and they are
going to do so on the basis of education. The proper question is what kind of a real future will their circumstances
allow them to make, and what part can education play in
helping bring that about?

Now all one has is the blind insistence of the people on
education and more education, an insistence that educators
seem to welcome as self-justification. And the youngsters
flood into the schools and out of them and finally a hundred
prepare signs and go and walk silently through Nimwes's
office, a stunning act in a society in which the young have
never questioned the old and the established structure. But
these are youngsters who are cut off equally from the island
life of the past and from the vision of the new that is inherent in the education given them. And they boil with frustration.

In 1973 the Trust Territory got its first mental-health
director, a post that seems long overdue. Dr. Robert Fisher,
a tall, genial, self-assured young man, travels through the
districts treating patients as well as monitoring mental
health programs. He is the first psychiatrist to examine
large numbers of Micronesians, and as we talked over a
reef-fish lunch at Saipan, the explanations of what he has
seen in an untapped field poured out.

"We're seeing a lot of problems associated with identity,"
he said. "This is the process, biological and emotional, in
which a young person starts sorting out who he is. And this
is done mostly through modeling, usually on someone in
whom he has an emotional interest. In the old Micronesia,
the models were clear. The emotional relationships were
obvious and so were the authority figures. But we [he refers
partly to the U.S. administration, partly to the new way]
have broken up the social contacts and reduced the biological value system—the extended family—and we have emas-
culated the chiefs. And the chiefs are saying, 'When we
were in charge we had things in control.' And now there is

no control, they say we can't cope, and that seems to be true. All this has been so abrupt. Kids have switched models, out of their own culture to those of the west. We must have the answer, it seems to them, we are in control, we have the money, we are the new way. But these kids can't shape value systems from the distorted picture they get of Americans. So in effect, we've created a void and we have made it hard for kids to learn how to live. It's not just progress, it's not so much that it happens, it's the way that it happens.

"Identity problems usually manifest themselves in stress, internal or external, often violence and misbehavior. The alcohol abuse here is amazing, the plain consumption of alcohol is amazing. This is most true in the district centers, where people seem most cut off from real life. Micronesians usually drink to get drunk, not to facilitate social intercourse. You see a lot of this among Micronesians who succeed, too—ulcers, hypertension, alcohol abuse all are very serious among Micronesians in government.

"Major mental disorders are as common here as on the mainland or anywhere in the world. I see a lot of schizo-paranoia and also schizo-affective, with reality testing impaired and a strong mood component, strong depressions. In districts where the culture calls for internalization, for self-effacement, and self-deprecation, the Marshalls, for instance, we see a lot of schizo-affective disorders and a lot of suicide, mostly among males, mostly associated with alcohol. I guess the Palauans are the closest to Americans, they're more competitive, more out-turned, but I see schizophrenia in the same volume there except that it projects outwards, it takes on paranoid overtones.

"I've seen more hysteria here than I've seen in my entire career. People paralyzed, blind, in pain that they usually relate to witchcraft, all the traditional neurotic patterns. There are lots of anxiety problems among Micronesians who achieve, but I do see hysteria at the village level too. You know, this is widely believed to be a form of neurotic relief in the least emerging cultures. . . .

"And I see lots of students in the boarding schools, the high schools. I think many of them have had psychotic decompensations from the effect of being away from their homes. They respond most effectively of all to being sent home. A lot of boarding students become psychotic.

"You know, the high schools take the kids and in effect become the homes, the parents, but they only take responsibility for education. But the child is severed from his home and his parents for months and even years. And this is the worst group of all, the group with the highest social dysfunction, the highest alcohol and suicide and violence rate. Boy, Micronesian high schools are a rough picture."

Life is dangerously unreal when its terms and opportunities and penalties do not relate directly to the capacities of the people who are involved. The American presence with its funding, its tendency to serve as a model and to set standards, its imposition of governmental and educational forms which are its own, its control and yet its lack of guidance, planning, or wisdom, obscures reality.

Everything about the islands, but the people and the implacable terrain, is institutionalized American—and badly done at that. Perhaps it is not fair to say we have sent our worst, but most certainly we have never sent our best, in terms of people or ideals or ideas. A whole body of knowledge has been developed on emerging nations, both in the State Department and around the world, and not a word of it has been sent here. Micronesia is a desert for ideas, with the sole exception of the democratic concept. The democratic idea in a modern world context—which in a broad sense is our great achievement—is a great gift to Micronesia (whether it is a practical gift is a slightly different question); but in the more immediate sense of solutions to problems, of practical ideas, of persuasive approaches, we have hardly bothered even to consider the need. Now that the fallacies of the last three decades are obvious to everyone, we have fallen back on the thought that after all, the Micronesians must chart their own future, that it would be neocolonialism for us to offer guidance. That may be true, despite what it says of the last three decades, but the problem is that the situation has deprived Micronesians of the bedrock of reality from which real and sound decisions are made.

The pressure of desperation, the struggle for something to eat, has shaped some Asian and some developing societies. Micronesia escaped that pressure, both as a primitive, subsistence society, and in its change into the modern world. No one argues that hunger is a desirable molder of character and attitude, but the problem is that change has come without pressure to respond to it in real ways. The fact that change is so rapid in Micronesia—from outer islands to district centers, from subsistence to cash, from dictatorship to democracy, from subservience to self-assertion, from communal to individual, from old customs to new desires, all in three decades—is not really the point. Change everywhere is rapid. Rather, as Dirk Ballendorf puts it, "This is a created society. They can't go forward on their own, but they can't go backward either." A created society is arbitrary, as opposed to one that evolves; it serves a vision, such as it is, that is not indigenous but of the creators; and its effect is to block the society that might have evolved in response to change had it been free to do so. I think that is the basic reason that despite the obviously increasing dissatisfaction of the people, no new forms seem to be developing.

And in such a situation, as Dr. Fisher might say, the maintenance of a firm identity is difficult, for a people and for individuals. In Palau, Tarkong Pedro said, "eight of ten children would rather be Americans. They feel Americans are fortunate. They are poor because they are Micronesians. That is what they see." They want to be as fortunate as Americans, but they find no alternatives open to them.

Ironically, this society's frustration does not seem to be limited to those on the outside looking in—it grips those inside the new money establishment as well. People seem dissatisfied with their jobs. They do not do a great deal of work and they resent the demand for schedules and regularity. Though in effect government workers are a privileged class, it is interesting to see the speed with which they leave their desks at four-thirty in the afternoon.

Thus the disparity of development, with political and educational development growing independently of economic development. That is part of the disparity in size and power between the United States and Micronesia. "The situation here," Father Hezel says, "is not at all like the classical patterns described by Barbara Ward and Myrdal and others. Here, with the metropolitan power, problems were overcome without even recognizing they were problems. 'Let there be education,' and lo, there was education." They were lifted falsely to a level where they cannot compete on their own merits.

Another critical point in the making of unreality is the absence not of a free press but of any press. With very minor exceptions, Micronesians are cut off from the information flow that is so basic to a world picture. There is a local radio station in each district which relies largely on American Forces Radio and Television material, including canned disc jockeys who apparently operate from California. There is a minimum of news and all of it comes over the government's telex system from Saipan. Called the Micronesian News Service, it appears surprisingly uncensored, but it certainly is not adequate news material. No wire service touches here. There are two small weeklies on Saipan and one very small weekly at Majuro whose editor, a former Peace Corps volunteer, focuses on local news and runs Micronesian News Service copy largely as filler. The radio stations pick up Voice of America and Armed Forces news, but no attempt is made to put it into perspective for the local audience. *The Pacific Daily News*, a comparatively good tabloid from Guam, comes in haphazardly by air but is read largely by expatriates. Again, when you are in the islands you find yourself wondering if the rest of the world really is out there, somewhere across the empty sea. People here could hardly be other than ignorant of the world and the way it works.

Now the conflicting thrusts of Micronesia seem to be coming to a head. The American contribution, having developed a momentum of expectation, is leveling out, but there is no way the people there can turn back. "We have reached—or passed—the point of no return. We must take our place in the world and the Pacific community," said Carl Heine. Thomas Remengesau, Distad at Palau, said sharply, "We cannot crawl back twenty-five years. If we were forced to do that, people would leave the islands—or the peso and the yen would be invited in." "They want things," Vitarelli said, "and you will lose if you try to persuade them otherwise. I also believe that they want the opportunity to earn for themselves—they do not want things given."

But just the same, they lack the wherewithall. The most striking physical thing about the islands, aside from their beauty, is the lack of the economic structure that people in developed countries take for granted. With that lack of infrastructure goes an ever greater lack of understanding of the nature of commerce, of capital accumulation, of how credit works and why schedules are important. Traders who ship to the islands are constantly in turmoil, for the ships are directed to the wrong places, the goods are pilfered on the docks, and Micronesian merchants do not pay their bills anyway. Shippers blame the Trust Territory government for many of their problems; and they probably are right in the sense that while it was expanding education and political insights, the government could have established a working structure for the handling of goods. But that still would have left the Micronesian attitude toward credit obligations. I talked to an Indian businessman from Hong Kong, agent for a textile firm, who was moving through the islands trying to collect bills of about $175,000. He would write off half of that, he said, but for the remainder he would sue, which would ruin the firms which owed him because then they would not be eligible for economic development loan funds. And he added, in a candid moment, "This is not my territory—normally I work Africa, and my predecessor here, he oversold, ten times as many shirts, for instance, as a store could hope to move. They have no idea, these merchants, what will sell and what won't and in what quantity."

Much more important than the lack of commercial knowledge—which could be improved—is the lack of resources, of which there really are only three areas—agriculture, marine resources, and services to tourists. Tourism is the chimera of everyone who looks at those sweeping beaches fringed by giant palms, but it is no more than that. For tourism to succeed, there must be hotels and things to do and an absence of people who swing machetes at passing vehicles. Around fifty thousand visitor-entries were made to Micronesia in 1973, for example, and about ninety percent were to the Marianas, which, with Guam, serves rather as Japan's Bermuda. The Marianas are separating, and there goes Micronesia's tourist industry. The other districts more or less split up the remaining ten percent, though this is deceptive too, since many visitors go to each district and are counted each time they land. I account for six tourists in the records of the year of my visit. Micronesia is proud of its beaches, but in this part of the world, as Petrus Tun pointed out, everything is ocean view and Micronesia is far away and difficult to reach for just another sight of the sea. Finally, the jobs that tourism produces tend to be low-level—if not menial—and not at all in keeping with Micronesia's view of itself. "Why should a people who have always seen themselves in the proud terms of self-sufficiency want to clean toilets for visitors?" a Micronesian leader asked.

The water is so deep around Micronesia that it is not as

rich a fishing ground as one might imagine. Nevertheless lots of tuna is taken in Micronesian waters, canned in Japan, and returned to Micronesia for sale to people who cannot afford it. Van Camp has a plant in Palau, but it freezes fish and sends them to Samoa because the United States charges a foreign import duty on goods arriving from Micronesia but not from Samoa. Micronesia has been struggling for years to get this relaxed, which would make its fish competitive in the American market, but it has never succeeded. It seems that the pressure of west-coast fishing interests is insurmountable. But the larger reason that Micronesia is not successful in the fishing industry is that Micronesians do not like to go to sea. Fishing is hard, lonely work on modern trawlers that go out for weeks at a time.

Micronesians do not like this, apparently for reasons that turn around both the cultural inheritance of the Micronesian people and their perceptions of today. They do not have a work ethic, do not honor work, and therefore consider work that is hard and long quite unpalatable. They are not lazy and shiftless in the western sense. When there is work to be done that they want to do they turn to with gusto. They just do not want to do it steadily. They want to stop in a bit and celebrate what they have done and have a party. Furthermore, they appear to be powerfully drawn to the emotional security inherent in the extended family and to the closeness of the island. They do not like to be away, as witness the "psychotic decompensations" that Fisher finds in boarding students. Neither do they like to be away for weeks on trawlers. Perhaps Koreans do not really like trawler duty any better than do Micronesians, but their alternatives are fewer. In Micronesia, it is always warm, "the taro patch is just outside and coconuts fall on the roof," in the words of Toshiro Paulis, who has spent a good part of his life trying to develop marine resources in Palau. Perhaps it would help if Micronesians owned the boats, Paulis thinks, but the crews still would not want to go out. After one trip, they would want to have a party. How about alternate crews? "Well, when one Micronesian goes to a party, everyone wants to go."

Obviously, fisheries, fish farming, shellfish, and canning have some potential, but its realization seems far off. The reasons are not so clear for the failure to develop at least a local fishing industry which could supply the centers in each district and cut down the Micronesian reliance on tuna imported from Japan. Cooperatives are one of the strong movements in Micronesia and in some places, particularly Ponape, they are working well. But the Marshall Islands High School imports a thousand pounds of fish weekly from Ponape because no Marshallese will guarantee the supply. The chief reason for the lack of a local fishing industry appears to be a failure of marketing, of planning, and of the necessary infrastructure.

Agriculture fails equally and for about the same reasons. Both Germany and Japan had plantations here, and some of the copra plantations the Germans planted are still bearing, though the trees are old and should be replaced. Making copra is very hard work and pays little even when the price of copra is up. More money could be made if copra was processed in Micronesia, but there is not enough to supply a plant that would convert it to oil and to other products. More than half of all Micronesia's copra comes from the Marshalls.

There is a ready market for vegetables, at U.S. bases and at Guam, as well as at the district centers. But if fishing is hard work, farming is more so—and lonely as well. Agricultural cooperatives are trying to organize markets, to buy fertilizer in bulk, and to own equipment in common, but they seem to get little help. Part of the problem is that much of the very limited land in Micronesia is still held by the Trust Territory government in the public domain; much of what remains is unworkable, and all of what is left is closely held and subject to the decisions of entire clans. It is not a situation which encourages the free-enterprise farmer, which has something to do with the startling sale of bell peppers from the school garden at Ponape.

Nor is free enterprise itself at all natural to Micronesians, though that is the system into which they have been brought. The extended-family system is a carry-over from the communal, subsistence past, and it continues to work with real force throughout Micronesia. Its obligations are many, including the duty to rally emotionally around any family member who is ill or who dies, no matter how far removed in blood ties or in geographic distance. Teachers, students, workers, officials, announce as a matter of course that they must go, and sometimes they are gone for a month. Alfonso Oiterong, education director at Palau, tightened his lips at this—it means important work must stop— but he said, "There is nothing I can do."

If the extended-family system works against the businessman, or the farmer who is expected to share his crop or the fisherman his catch, it is most disruptive of all to the person who has made the transition to a cash job. For he too is expected to supply bits of money more or less on demand to his own far-reaching family and to that of his wife. Whoever has is expected to give, and whoever has more, to give more. This is not leeching but simply a replaying of what life has always been. Those who demand do so in part because they have paid their dues, they have earned title to the obligation they impose. In Palau and elsewhere there is an intricate system usually known only as "customs" which amounts to a sort of mental ledger tally of each obligation. When one helps another it is a score, it will be remembered, sooner or later it must be repaid. Often it is paid in food which the person in a subsistence economy grows or catches and then cooks, but which the person employed by the government must buy.

"Sometimes," said Leonardo Ruluked, who is principal of Palau High School, "you want to tell them to forget it, to leave you alone, that they don't understand, it isn't that way anymore." A dark look passed over his sunny face. "I thought of that, but you don't do that. On the island, everybody knows, and then you are alone. And, you know, if your child dies, you go and bury your child alone, you and your wife . . ."

The shattering effect of introducing money into a subsistence economy is that it shifts the focus of the society from the group to the individual. Chutomu Nimwes suggests that this has already happened at Truk, but I believe that he is identifying only the beginning. Many societies are undergoing this, of course, but the Micronesian situation is complicated by the imposed unreality.

It is true, for instance, that the work attitudes of the old society are inconsistent with the demands of the new society, but the equation goes a step further. Carl Heine agrees that "we don't want to dirty our hands," but he discounts much of the theory of the old work habits. Micronesians always worked hard when it was necessary, and he sees no reason that they could not or would not adapt to a new work form if they thought it was necessary. But they don't, he believes, because the training implicit in the course that society has taken has made physical work seem demeaning and has exalted office work.

Perhaps Heine's anger leads him to overstatement, but there is a germ of truth in the idea. It is simply a disgrace that the new high school being built at Jaluit in the Marshalls is being done entirely by Korean skilled labor. I met the project manager on a Majuro beach and asked him how many Marshallese he employed. Oh, many, he said, to lift and carry, but not to do real work. Not that it mattered to him, he said, carefully choosing his English, he would be pleased to bring only designers from Korea and use all Marshallese if any with skills were available. But they aren't, and furthermore, they're not reliable, he said, they don't come to work for days at a time. It does not matter with common laborers, but to have someone like a special electrician disappear at a critical moment, well, shaking his head at the thought, that would be disastrous.

Certainly the new elite are government workers. The men wear clean shirts and trousers and *zoris,* and the women wear flowered dresses and *zoris* and on Fridays they wear long island dresses and flowers in their hair, and they work with papers which common folk cannot even understand, and they never sweat at their labor because the airconditioner is always on. That is how the Americans do it, and that is how the successful Micronesians do it. And when you come down to it, that is what the academic model American schools teach their students to admire and to expect.

None of these facts is mysterious. They are all well known and indeed, become obvious after a glance at the export-import figures and at the nature of the economy, and talks with a few Micronesians. No one advertises the facts, but no one denies them either. Micronesians are fundamentally interested in face, which may be why they patiently let the visitor work through his own discoveries, agreeing quietly as he leads them step by step through the details of their own disaster.

It is more startling, however, when the newcomer realizes that Americans also have understood the Micronesian dilemma all along. They have understood the common Micronesian work attitudes and cultural patterns. They have certainly recognized the weakness of the economy. And they have understood what would happen to the people there if they were inundated in money.

The best anthropological study ever made in Micronesia was the Navy's extensive effort just after World War II. Young anthropologists who began in that survey today are the leading experts on Pacific cultures. Anthropology may be one of those fields in which the more you learn the less you know, but certainly the implications of life on a small island in the security of a plentiful and non-threatening environment is well understood. Despite their small size, Micronesian cultures are diverse and men who understand them resist the easy generalizations that fall so naturally from the journalist's typewriter. But just the same, they are not mystified by the Micronesian attitude toward bucking a plow or spending months in grinding labor at sea or swabbing out a hotel bathroom.

And westerners certainly have understood the failures of the Micronesian economy, so long have they been trying to make something from it. One of the earliest recorded economic commentaries came in rude English from a Chinese who landed in Palau in 1783 with a British skipper: "This is a very poor place and very poor people no got clothes, no got rice, no got hog, no got nothing only yams, little fish and cocoa-nut; no got nothing make trade, very little make eat."* Things have not improved much since. The Spanish ignored the issue, the Germans failed at it, the Japanese succeeded only with a controlled market and a system of serfdom, and the Americans have played with the subject. From the beginning of the American tenure, there were desultory efforts to improve the economy, usually accompanied by considerable rhetoric. But the Director of Coconut Operations, try as he may have done, did not increase copra production. The old trees are still there and people are still husking the nuts on a stick and peeling out the meat with a curved knife and the copra is still sent in bulk to Japan where the processing money is made. There is no technology, in this technological age, that can make the handling of coconut oil profitable on a small scale.

The agricultural experiments generally have come to naught, the cacao seedlings withering, the white pepper of Ponape still negligible, the potential vegetable fields unplanted. Neither education nor other government effort has spent much time on the most promising economic form in Micronesia, the workers' cooperative. The shipping and transport on which island commerce obviously depends has been allowed to creak from one disaster to another with

---

* From *The History of Prince Lee Boo* (London: Thomas Hughes, 1823), cited by Howard Seay and Dirk Ballendorf in an unpublished manuscript, "Sense and Nonsense in Micronesia."

bankrupt firms and repossessed ships littering the economic history of the period. Very little effort has been made toward developing capital or even toward an understanding of credit systems. Warehousing is still inadequate. International merchants still bombard the Trust Territory government with descriptions of their losses from various governmental and infrastructural failures. Insurance rates are still prohibitively high. All this seems to baffle the American planners, who cling instead to their hopes of tourism as the panacea. Look at all those beautiful beaches, they keep saying. On a couple of occasions they invited high-powered research firms from the States to look at the situation, and after each visit they received book-length reports, but nothing much seemed to change.

The measure of the real American effort lies in the innocuous matter of the duty imposed on canned fish products from Micronesia, which American officials cannot persuade the Congress to lift. It is the first time you realize that west-coast fishermen constitute a great American power bloc.

And it is useful to remember that throughout this period, the United States has devoted billions of dollars to improving underdeveloped economies all over the world. Even today the Agency for International Development is letting contracts for this or that improvement wherever in the world American interests seem to be involved. The Secretary of State went before the United Nations with an elaborate proposal for world cooperation on improving the share which the have-nots of the world take of its commerce. But in Micronesia, the problems have been insurmountable.

Against this background, I found it still more startling to realize that American planners have understood all along the penalty for introducing money and education and political development without a supporting economic base. The most important of the many statements that show American understanding of the situation was made by Anthony Solomon in his report to the President. Solomon had an economic background. He went to Micronesia with a presidential mandate to study the situation and he placed his report in the President's hands. The report became an official working paper of the National Security Council and through national security action memoranda it became a part of American policy for Micronesia. Writing almost a decade-and-a-half ago, Solomon spelled it out with relentless precision:

> Despite the importance of subsistence production in Micronesia, there is a growing desire for money income to use for purchasing wanted imports. In many areas a taste has been cultivated for rice, sugar, tobacco, beer and other items typically consumed in market economies; and outboard motors, motor scooters, gasoline and kerosene are rapidly becoming "necessities" in and around the district centers of Micronesia. Largely because it is viewed as a channel to desirable employment and higher money incomes, more and better education is everywhere extolled and is widely coveted by the young.
>
> Subsistence production can support adequate living standards only so long as land resources are ample. Rapidly growing population . . . is beginning to press against land resources in some parts of Micronesia. Throughout the Trust Territory the population density is only 121 per square mile; but several large volcanic islands, now virtually inaccessible in the interior, account for most of the unused land. On some coral atolls in the Truk District rural population densities exceed 500 per square mile. With one of the fastest growing populations in the world, living standards in Micronesia may well fall in the coming years. . . . A two-pronged program which will raise productivity and facilitate mobility is required to prevent the number of people from outrunning the availability of productive resources.
>
> Proper education plays a critical role in any program

for economic development. Education is necessary to provide the minimum skills required to raise productivity. . . . But greater education in turn will stimulate further the demand for money incomes and imported goods. Secondary education at boarding schools attracts teen-agers from the rural into the urban and semi-urban centers . . . and exposes them to a way of life substantially different from that to which they are accustomed. The same education which prepares Micronesians for absorption into the modern world often generates dissatisfaction and impatience with traditional modes of existence. The students become too sophisticated in their tastes to go "back to the farm." An expanded and improved educational system will, unless care is taken to prevent it, increase not only the desire for more cash but will raise unrealizable expectations for salaried employment.

While secondary education . . . prepares students for more modern life and more modern employment, it does not automatically provide them with jobs. The demand for better educated Micronesians will not rise spontaneously to absorb the increased supply of them. Unless jobs are available for graduating students—or unless the educational program is designed to discourage unrealistic expectations for salaried employment— many reasonably well-educated students will be disappointed when they reach the job market. Already in Palau there are substantial numbers of men and women willing to work but unable to find jobs, and in Ponape and Truk "urban" unemployment in the District Centers is reported as beginning to appear.*

Perhaps the final step in the Micronesian economic disaster was the decision to raise salaries toward the American civil service scale. The first step came when High Commis-

* U.S. Government, *The Economic and Social Development of Micronesia,* Special Report to the President by Anthony Solomon, 1963. Vol. 2, pp. 2–5.

sioner Goding decided, as Tom Gilliland put it, "that it was just socially irresponsible" to pay laborers twenty-two cents an hour, and raised the basic scale to fifty cents. At that moment, cutting copra, Micronesia's only export crop, became a disadvantaged occupation, since there was no way the hot, tedious work with the machete could earn more than half the lowest government scale.

After status negotiations began and the Nixon administration brought Ambassador Williams to the task, Micronesian salaries shot up rapidly. Robert Mangan believes that from then on the administration lost interest in economic development and focused on that plebiscite to come, and John Carver thinks that the administration's approach at this point was that "we'll buy our way into their good graces."

Whatever the reasoning, the salary expansion raised Micronesians toward American standards. Figures posted in the Marshall Islands in 1973, for example, showed clerk-typists drawing from $1,500 to $3,000 a year; surveyors from $3,000 to $7,000; an electrician at $3,370; a police captain at $6,074; nurses at $3,000; elementary teachers at $3,500 to $4,000; and high school teachers at considerably more. Anko Billy, he of the struggling English, earned $3,578, and the district administrator, Oscar de Brum, earned $24,000.

Naturally an ever greater portion of the budget went for salaries, and since the budgets then were leveling off, an ever lesser portion went for the kind of development that leads to a sound economy. But more important, learning to live on such salaries priced Micronesians right out of the Asian labor market. It is hard to argue that the sweatshops of Asia are desirable or that Micronesians should have been held to such wages, but the fact remains that there is no way in the Asian context that Micronesians can support the living style and income expectations that the American-inspired salaries have given them.

In the end, this may be the point that allows the United States to have its way with Micronesia.

Educators recognize—as well as anyone—the lack of reality in which their policies have helped mire Micronesians. Thet do not know what to do about it, or what they might have done differently at any particular point. It is one of the few questions that ruffle David Ramarui's calm, and he takes refuge in defining the problem very narrowly as graduates without jobs, and therefore can say that it is not the role of education to supply jobs. Educators who do want to move in new directions are impaled on the continuing shrinkage of the discretionary side of their budgets. At Palau, Alfonso Oiterong dreamed of a culture-oriented school that would combine work and learning in new ways. It seemed to have promise of something that might break the downward trend, but headquarters told him to forget it, there was no money for it.

The situation in private schools is just as unhappy and as baffling. In her school at Palau, Sister Martha Ramarui said with some anguish, "If I could choose, I would close the schools and do something more useful." Rather glowingly she described a system she had seen in Singapore with the first six grades alike, the next three streamed toward interests that were usually vocational, and the last three tightly focused on a vocation. But the parents of her children, she added, would never accept such deviation.

The Micronesian Seminar, headed by Francis Hezel at Truk held a conference called Education for What? to echo the phrase on so many educators' lips. When I read the report of the week-long discussion, I was reminded of the board of education at Yap. The participants raised questions but found no answers, and there was throughout the inordinate concern for the feelings of others that permeates this society. It did establish beyond question, however, that no one knows what to do.

It does not seem education's obligation single-handedly to chart the course of a nation, if Micronesia is to be a nation. That should be a matter of consensus developing among the people for political leaders and educators alike to

follow. But that process is short-circuited here by the separation of terrain, by the ambivalent attitude of the people
toward politics (torn as they are between the old and the
new), and by the ambivalent attitude of the politicians
themselves (torn as they are between nationalism on the
one hand and the fact, on the other, that Americans still
hold the real power). And the process is made more difficult
by the fact—however dimly it now is recognized—that to
put things on a realistic basis is going to bruise many people's hopes and assumptions about what society owes
them.

And yet, education has hurried people down the wrong
path, leading them further and further from workable solutions. So it does seem that education could do some things
differently, at the risk of some parental outrage, and perhaps stir some new sense of reality into the equation. Following, therefore, are a few suggestions. They are not solutions—there are no solutions just now—but they are
sensible, and after years of the nonsensical might be refreshing.

First, however, it is worth noting that there are some
things that would improve the reality quotient simply by
improving the existing system. Better trained teachers
would make better students, and teachers who spoke English would be better English teachers. Micronesia needs a
universal language, presumably in terms of nationhood,
certainly in terms of relating to the rest of the world. The
schools need a locally published curriculum that focuses on
what for these children is the center of the world, and then
relates it to the rest of the world in clear terms. There
should be a much more fully developed cultural curriculum,
and some of it should be published in English so it can be
used in all schools. It may be difficult to build a body of
vernacular literature, but it would not be so hard to develop
a body of Micronesian-based literature. If reading material
was developed and reading teaching expanded, actual reading might follow. I keep thinking of the run on those Nancy

Drew books. Reading leads to libraries, and libraries bring the world's knowledge, for which Micronesia is in particularly great need. At the same time, a genuinely free press, probably using radio, should be developed with funding independent of the Trust Territory government. It should put special emphasis on news and news background stories from around the world, well translated into each district's language. Micronesians will never know the world without a free press.

When the course is so firmly set, suggestions for real change tend to take on an autocratic note, which both the consensus approach to life and rankling memories of the Japanese dictatorship make unpalatable in Micronesia. But just the same, there does seem to be a good deal of confusion on the islands about what democracy really means. The sense that every person should have an equal opportunity to compete, for example, has been transmogrified into the feeling that everyone should have the right to succeed. It is not really a matter of democratic principle that everyone should go to high school. To choose only a few would not be inconsistent if the choice was fair and especially if there were valid work alternatives for those not chosen. And if this is obvious, it only serves to point up the confusion.

I think Micronesia has too many high schools and too many high-school students and too many graduates. Sometimes the Congress of Micronesia lists universal education to the twelfth grade as a goal, which is a dreadful mistake. The territory spends too much of its education money on boarding those high school students, and on their desultory education.

But even more important, the education is destructive. Severed from their past and unequipped for a real future, naturally these young graduates are full of uncertain anguish that is building toward rage. Why not? They have been cheated, the promises made them are fraudulent, the basis of their selves is eroded, their lives are corrupted, and they are discovering all this. It would be much better to close the high schools in each district and devote the money saved to two aims. The first should be to improve the elementary schools, with emphasis on language, reading, and vocational education, which is now unknown at the elementary level.

The second aim should be to reopen a single Pacific Islands Central School and make it truly excellent in a way that the old PICS never was. It should be located on Truk, to interact with Xavier and for its central location. It should seek the intellectual elite of the islands by the fairest possible examination and each year take a limited number, perhaps fifty boys and fifty girls. It should be conducted entirely in English, should have mastery of English as one of its primary aims, and should have a frankly academic orientation with its students aimed toward college abroad. It should last five years, with a sixth year if necessary for college preparation, and it should be prepared to send its students home at reasonable intervals to avoid those psychotic decompensations.

Of course this would produce an educated governmental and managerial elite, but then, that already exists.

Next, each district should open a small vocational high school modeled on Father Costigan's Ponape Agricultural and Trade School. They should be started and operated in close conjunction with workers' cooperatives, which should be emphasized independently of education. This surely is the economic form most suited to the communal cultural background and to the lack of capital. If any system is likely to overcome the Micronesian distaste for steady, scheduled work and for working for another person, it is likely to be a flexible cooperative in which he can set his own time and he can feel he is working for himself. There is reason to think this would work. Cooperatives at Ponape are successful, partly because of Costigan's pioneering efforts. At Palau the elementary-school fair which sells agricultural products is such a success that for two months before it starts the kids can think of nothing else.

The government should begin seriously to subsidize communal agriculture and fishing projects that would aim at making Micronesians self-sufficient in fish and vegetables at least, and perhaps able to supply the large American community at Guam and at Kwajalein. The vocational schools could become part of this effort, loaning equipment and materials, supplying expertise from trained teachers, and turning out students geared to the specific needs of specific cooperatives. In addition to fishing and agriculture, cooperatives and schools should stress construction and mechanics.

The point, of course, is practicality and reality. All of these concepts, language and libraries and an academic high school and vocational schools and cooperatives, turn around presenting the realities of the world. Work is a necessary prerequisite to receiving goods in every social form. Oil production does affect the price of rice, the politics of emerging nations do apply to Micronesia, détente does relate to the strategic realities of the Pacific and thus to Micronesians. Micronesians are very intelligent people, and if such information was worked into their education in a meaningful way, it would not be lost on them.

Obviously I am not suggesting that such simple actions would turn the situation around. But still, if education has led people away from reality, why shouldn't it begin to lead them back? The move would depend on people's thinking changing, and the process of trying to bring it about might start that change, which really is the key question in Micronesia's future. And with the onset of a little reality, perhaps it would prove infectious. Perhaps the pleasure of putting one's feet on the ground and facing one's future with eyes open would be so great that people would want more.

Starting such movement would require a will not yet present on the American side and leadership not yet present on the Micronesian side. But still, one can only whistle in the dark for so long. Reality will intrude eventually, constructively or destructively, and the restlessness and the lurking sense of danger there suggests the time may not be far off. And then, unless the transfer from unreal to real is handled with a wisdom never before seen in Micronesia, the bills for the last thirty years will be presented for payment.

SOURCES

The American Touch in Micronesia depends primarily on interviews, with sources of quotations made evident in the text. I also have made a reasonably thorough search of the books and articles that pertain specifically to my interests, though I have made no attempt to assemble a complete bibliography on Micronesia. The bulk of material generally available on Micronesia is in cultural matters, with a lesser body in strategic and political affairs.

The most helpful periodicals were the *Congressional Record* and the *New York Times*. Others that were useful include *Education Daily, Pacific Daily News* (Guam), *Honolulu Advertiser, Washington Post, Washington Star, Wall Street Journal, Christian Science Monitor,* and *Chicago Tribune. The Micronesian Reporter* is a government-sponsored quarterly offering a wealth of well-written, well-edited information.

Specific citations include:

William H. Alkire, *An Introduction to the Peoples and Cultures of Micronesia* (Addison-Wesley Modular Publications, Module 18, 1972), pp. 1–56.

Elizabeth Kelley Antilla, *A History of The People of the Trust Territory of the Pacific Islands and Their Education,* doctoral dissertation submitted to the University of Texas, 1965 (Ann Arbor: University Microfilms).

Hanson W. Baldwin, "Keys to The Pacific," *Reader's Digest,* December 1971.

Dirk A. Ballendorf, "Catalysts or Barnacles in Micronesia: The First Five Years of the Peace Corps," in Frank P. King, ed., *Oceania and Beyond: Essays on The Pacific Since 1945* (Westport, Conn.: Greenwood Press, 1976).

———, "The Hardest Fight," *Micronesian Reporter,* First Quarter, 1969.

———, "Japanese Bastion in the Pacific," *Micronesian Reporter,* First Quarter, 1972.

———, "America's Trusteeship in Micronesia as A Development Administration," ms. submitted to Harvard University, 1969.

———, "Coming Full Circle: A New School for Micronesia," *British Journal of Educational Technology* 5, no. 2 (May 1974).

———, "Historic and Cultural Preservation in Micronesia," *Micronesian Reporter,* Third Quarter, 1975.

Vicente T. Blaz, Lt. Col., U. S. Marine Corps and Samuel S. H. Lee, "The Cross of Micronesia," *Naval War College Review,* June 1971.

David Boorstin, *Changing Status of Micronesia,* Editorial Research Reports I, no. 21, 6 June, 1975.

Edwin H. Bryan, Jr., "Geography of the Trust territory," in *Basic Information, Trust Territory of the Pacific Islands* (Honolulu: Trust Territory of the Pacific Islands, 1951).

Nat Joseph Colletta, *American Schools for the Natives of Ponape,* doctoral thesis submitted to the University of Michigan, 1972 (Ann Arbor: University Microfilms).

Congress of Micronesia, multiple documents.

Stanley A. de Smith, *Microstates and Micronesia: Problems of America's Pacific Islands and Other Minute Territories* (New York: New York University Press, 1970).

Edward Dodd, *Polynesian Seafaring* (New York: Dodd, Mead, 1972).

I. G. Edmonds, *Micronesia, America's Outpost in the Pacific* (New York: Bobbs-Merrill, 1974).

Kenneth P. Emory, "Kapingamarangi, Social and Religious Life on a Polynesian Atoll," Honolulu: *Bernice P. Bishop Museum Bulletin 228* (1965).

Robert Gibson, "Trust Territory: Cultural Education and Westernized Schooling," unpublished ms.

Thomas Gladwin, *East Is A Big Bird* (Cambridge: Harvard University Press, 1970).

Carl Heine, *Micronesia at The Crossroads* (Honolulu: University Press of Hawaii, 1974).

Francis X. Hezel, S.J., "In Search of A Home: Colonial Education in Micronesia," Moen, Truk: Micronesian Seminar, 1974.

————, "Micronesia's Education for Self-Government: Frolicking in the Backyard," Moen, Truk: Micronesian Seminar, 1974.

E. J. Kahn, Jr., *A Reporter in Micronesia* (New York: Norton, 1966).

Donald F. McHenry, *Micronesia, Trust Betrayed* (Washington, D.C.: Carnegie Endowment for International Peace, 1975).

Norman Meller, *The Congress of Micronesia* (Honolulu: University of Hawaii Press, 1969).

Nancy Modiano, William L. Leap and Rudolph C. Troike, *Recommendations for Language Policy in Indian Education* (Washington, D.C.: Center for Applied Linguistics, 1973).

Stephen C. Murray, "Meanwhile, Down in The Classroom," unpublished ms.

James W. Ney and Donella K. Eberle, "Selected Bibliographies: Bilingual/Bicultural Education," *The Linguistic Reporter*, January 1975.

Don Oberdorfer, "America's Neglected Colonial Paradise," *Saturday Evening Post*, 29 February, 1964.

Public Papers of the Presidents, John F. Kennedy, 1962 (Washington, D.C.: Government Printing Office, 1963).

Philip W. Quigg, "Coming of Age in Micronesia," *Foreign Affairs*, April 1969.

A. M. Rosenthal, "U. S. Gives Hope to Pacific Isles," *New York Times*, 12 February, 1962.

Muriel R. Saville and Rudolph C. Troike, *A Handbook of Bilingual Education* (Washington, D.C.: Teachers of English to Speakers of Other Languages, revised edition, 1975).

Howard Seay and Dirk A. Ballendorf, "Sense and Nonsense in Micronesia," unpublished ms.

John Singleton, "Education, Planning and Political Development in Micronesia," in Daniel T. Hughes and Sherwood G. Lingenfelter, eds., *Political Development in Micronesia* (Columbus: Ohio State University Press, 1974).

Bernard Spolsky, "South Pacific Conference on Bilingual Education," *The Linguistic Reporter*, April 1975.

J. L. Taylor, Lt. Cmdr., USNR, "Education in the Trust Territory," in *Basic Information, Trust Territory of the Pacific Islands* (Honolulu: Trust Territory of the Pacific Islands, 1951).

Donald M. Topping, "Bilingual Education Program for Micronesia," *The Linguistic Reporter*, May/June 1975.

Harry S. Truman, *Memoirs, Vol. I: Year of Decisions* (Garden City, N.Y.: Doubleday, 1955).

Robert Trumbull, *Paradise in Trust: A Report on Americans in Micronesia, 1946–1951* (New York: Sloane, 1959).

Trust Territory of the Pacific Islands, *Annual Reports to the Secretary of Interior*, 1952–1974 (Honolulu/Guam/Saipan).

————, *Manual of Administration*, 2 vols., Saipan, 1964.

U.S. Congress. House of Representatives. Committee on Appropriations. *Hearings before a Subcommittee: Department of the Interior and Related Agencies Appropriations; for fiscal years since 1952.*

U. S. Congress. U. S. Senate. Same citation as above.

U. S. Department of State, *Annual Reports to the United Nations on the Administration of the Trust Territory of the Pacific Islands,* 1948–1974.

U. S. Government. *The Economic and Social Development of Micronesia.* Special Report to the President by Anthony Solomon, 1963.

Ruth G. Van Cleve, *The Office of Territorial Affairs* (New York: Praeger, 1974).

James M. Vincent, ed., *Micronesia's Yesterday* (Saipan: Trust Territory Department of Education, 1973).

Dexter Waugh and Bruce Koon, "Breakthrough for Bilingual Education," *Civil Rights Digest*, Summer 1974.

James H. Webb, Capt., U. S. Marine Corps, "Turmoil in Paradise: Micronesia at the Crossroads," *U. S. Naval Institute Proceedings*, July 1972.

Robert Wenkham (with text by Byron Baker), *Micronesia, The Breadfruit Revolution* (second printing) (Honolulu: University Press of Hawaii, 1972).

————, *The Great Pacific Rip-Off, Corporate Rape in The Far East* (Chicago: Follett, 1974).

H. J. Wiens, *Pacific Island Bastions of the United States* (New York: Van Nostrand, 1962).

INDEX